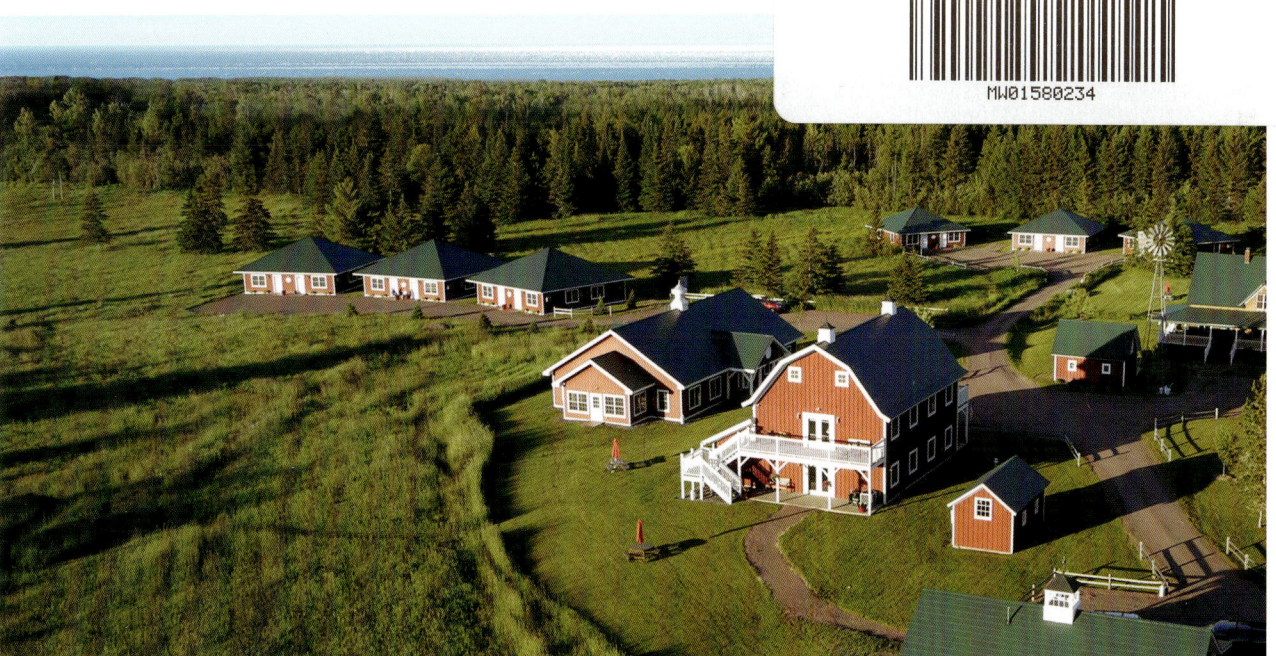

Madeline Island School of the Arts (MISA) is a top ranked, nationally recognized school that offers 5-day workshops from June through October in photography, painting. writing, quilting and fiber arts.

The campus facilities, which include studios, lodging and dining, were built between 2010 and 2012 on the site of the former Sandstrom Dairy Farm. Only the farmhouse was kept from the original farm which began serving the community in the early 1900s.

Madeline Island is one of the twenty-two Apostle Islands and provides exceptional opportunities for nature photography. The highlight of all photography workshops are trips to the famous Lake Superior Sea Caves located on Devil and Sand Islands.

We hope you enjoy these wonderful images of our area.

Madeline Island School of the Arts • 978 Middle Road, PO Box 536, La Pointe WI 54850 • www.madelineschool.com

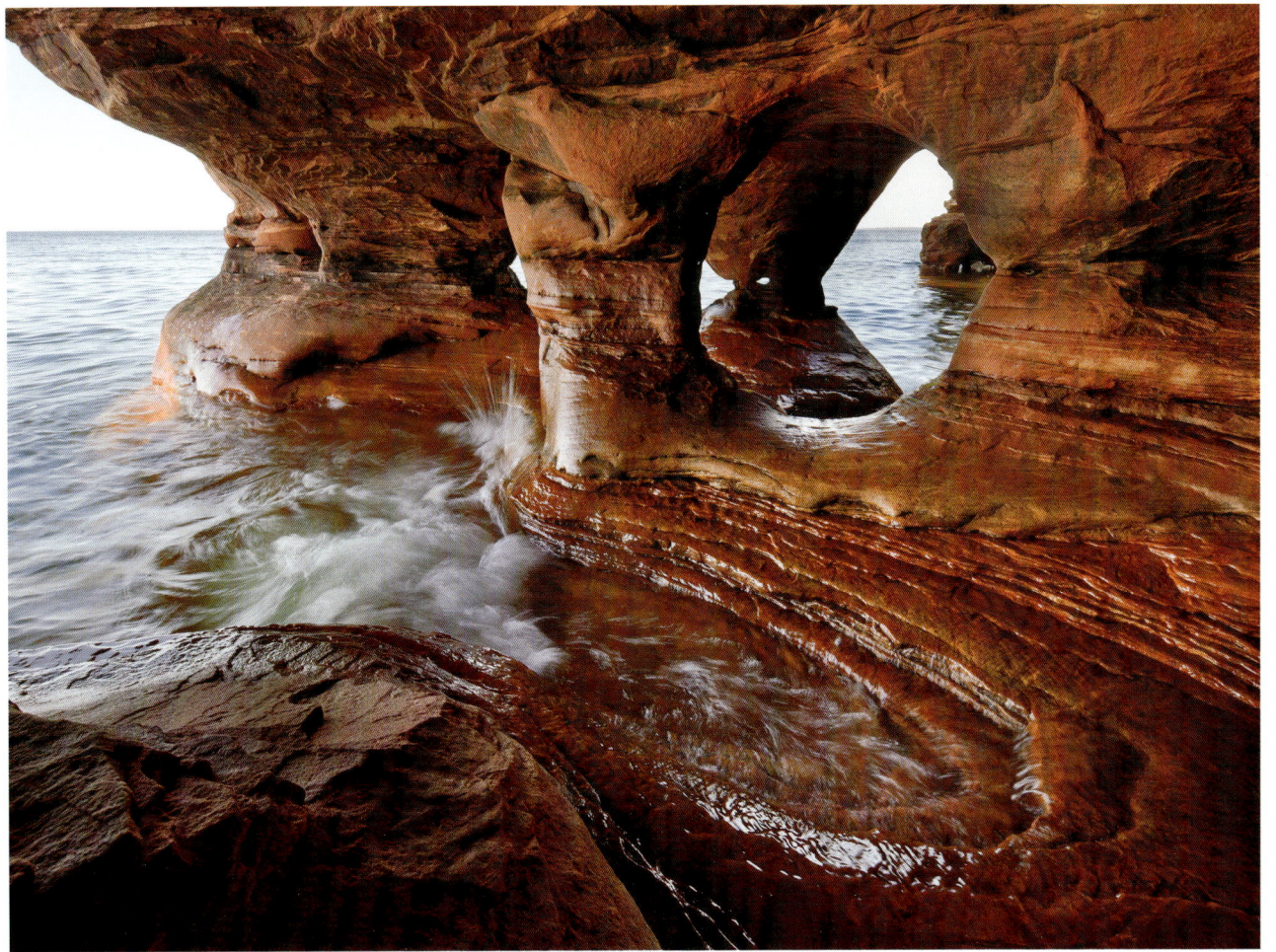

Devils Island, Apostle Islands National Lakeshore

Plate 1

APOSTLE ISLANDS

From Land and Sea — Souvenir Edition

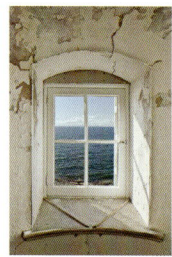

© 2012 Craig Blacklock

ISBN 978-1-892472-26-7

Second printing, April, 2017

Published by
Blacklock Photography Galleries
521 Folz Blvd., Moose Lake, MN 55767
www.blacklockgallery.com • 1-888-485-0478

Printed in Canada by Friesens—text paper FSC certified

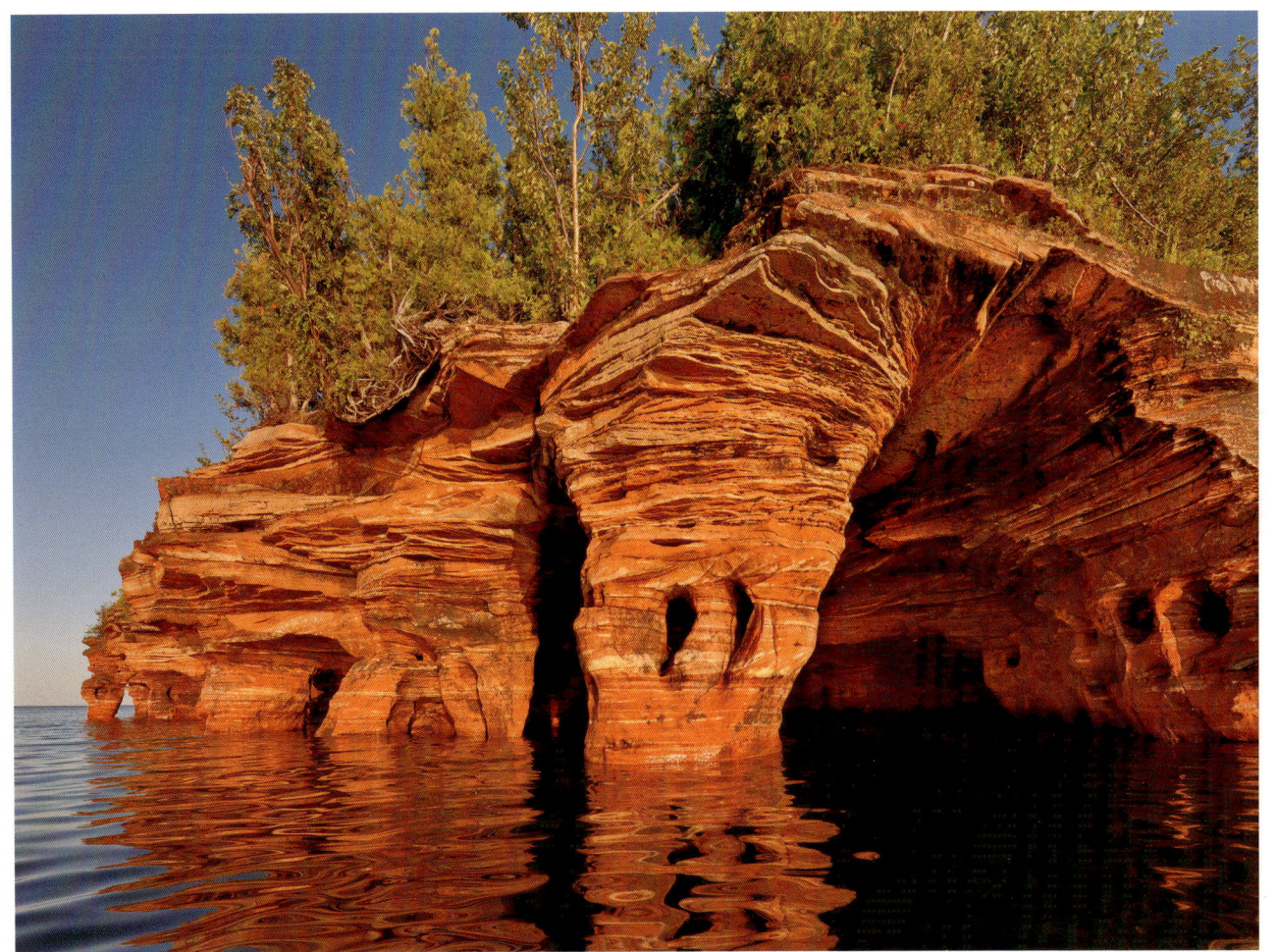

Devils Island, Apostle Islands National Lakeshore

Plate 2

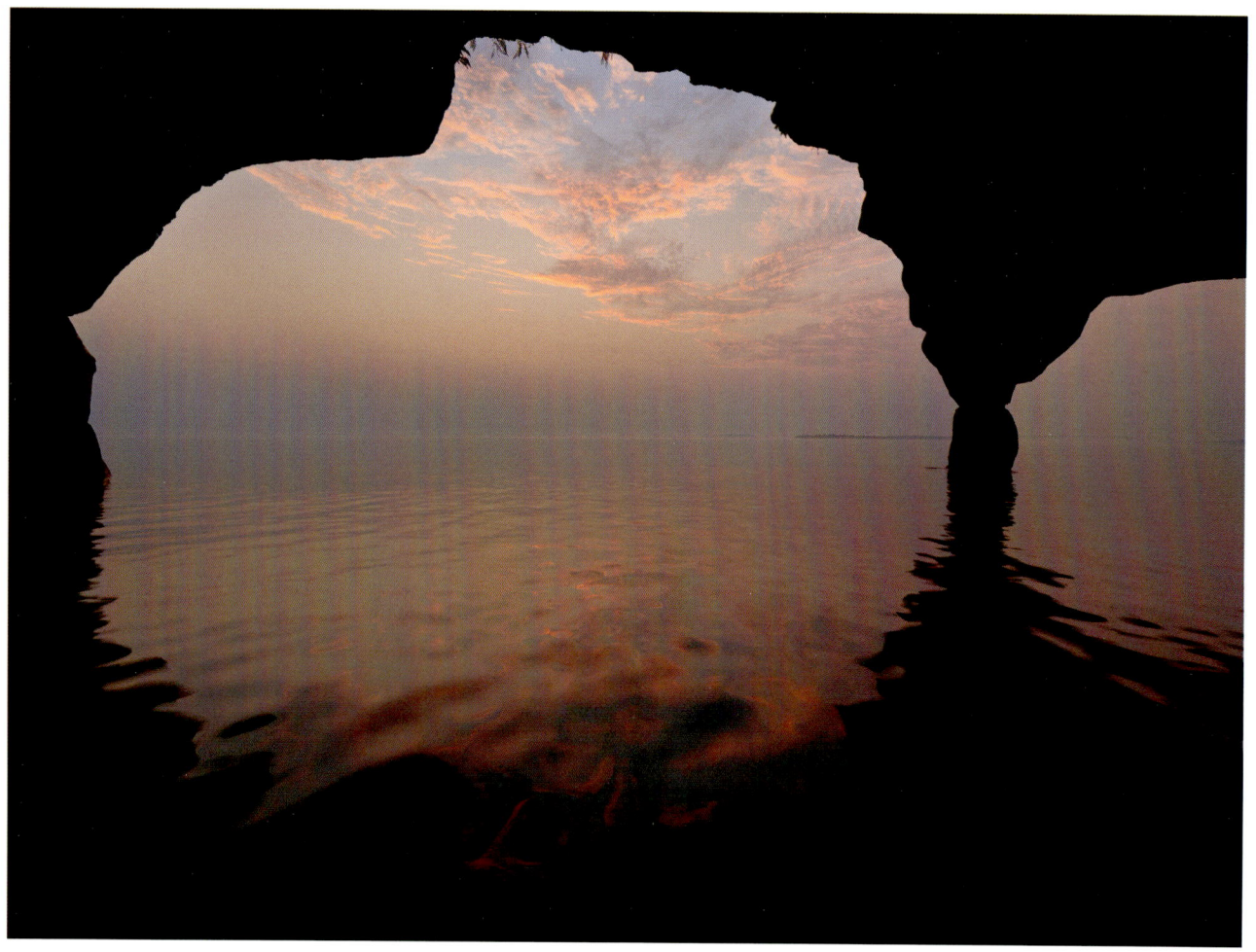

Sand Island, Apostle Islands National Lakeshore

Plate 3

For 12,000 years, Lake Superior and its post-glacial predecessors have been sculpting the Apostle Islands' 600 million-year-old Precambrian sandstone, producing extensive stretches of sea caves and arches on the mainland at Mawikwe Bay, and on Sand, Bear, and Devils Islands. Other interesting landforms, such as clay banks, sand spits, tombolos, sand dunes, barrier beaches, and lagoons have developed throughout the islands.

Native Americans came to the Apostles almost as soon as the islands emerged from the glacial meltwater. Prior to Europeans coming to North America, the Ojibwe, the tribe occupying the islands most recently, lived on the East Coast. An important part of Ojibwe history is their multi-generational migration into the western Great Lakes. Around 1395, many settled on *Moningwanekaaniing* (Madeline Island)—the cultural and spiritual center for the region's Ojibwe. Moningwanekaaniing means *place of the golden-breasted woodpecker* (northern flicker).

European influence in the area increased when French fur traders established a trading post on Madeline Island in 1693. By 1834 the era of the Voyageurs was in decline, and the first commercial fishing venture was started at La Pointe, on Madeline Island. In 1854, on Madeline Island, the Minnesota and Lake Superior Ojibwe signed a treaty establishing permanent reservations within their ancestral homeland.

The Soo Locks opened in 1855, ushering in commercial shipping, and the first Apostle Islands lighthouses were built in 1856 and 1857. Beginning in the 1860s, brownstone quarrying, logging, and farming impacted most islands, but diminished over time, and the island forests began to cover the evidence of human activity.

People wanting to escape the heat of the cities found the Apostles a refreshing get-away—so many, that it became necessary to protect the islands from development. The Apostle Islands National Lakeshore was established in 1970. By 1986, it included all but Madeline Island, which is partially protected by Big Bay State Park, Big Bay Town Park, and the Madeline Island Wilderness Preserve. In 2004, eighty percent of the Apostle Islands National Lakeshore was given the extra designation of federally protected wilderness. To honor the man most responsible for protecting the islands, this was named the Gaylord Nelson Wilderness.

Except for 12 miles of mainland shoreline, the entire park is made up of islands—thus a boat is essential for getting around. If you don't have your own boat, several services can be found in and around Bayfield. It is important to remember that Superior's waters are cold enough to cause hypothermia any time of the year, and calm waters can quickly turn into dangerous waves in minutes. Proper equipment, training, and common sense are all essential for safe boating.

I hope my images will help keep your memories alive, allow you to better share stories with friends, lead you to seek new adventures—and above all, inspire you to work to protect our nation's natural and cultural heritage.

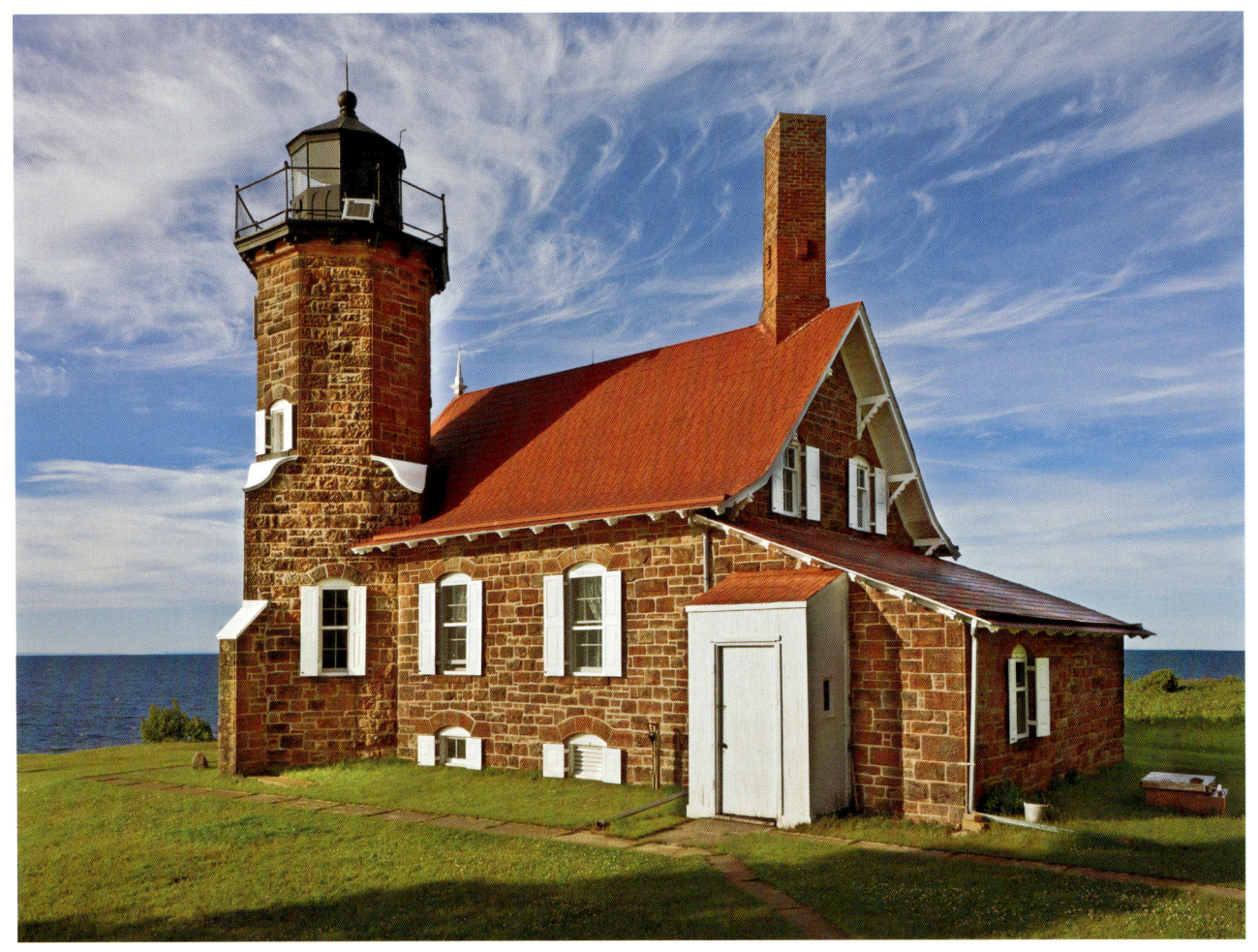

Sand Island Lighthouse, Apostle Islands National Lakeshore

Plate 4

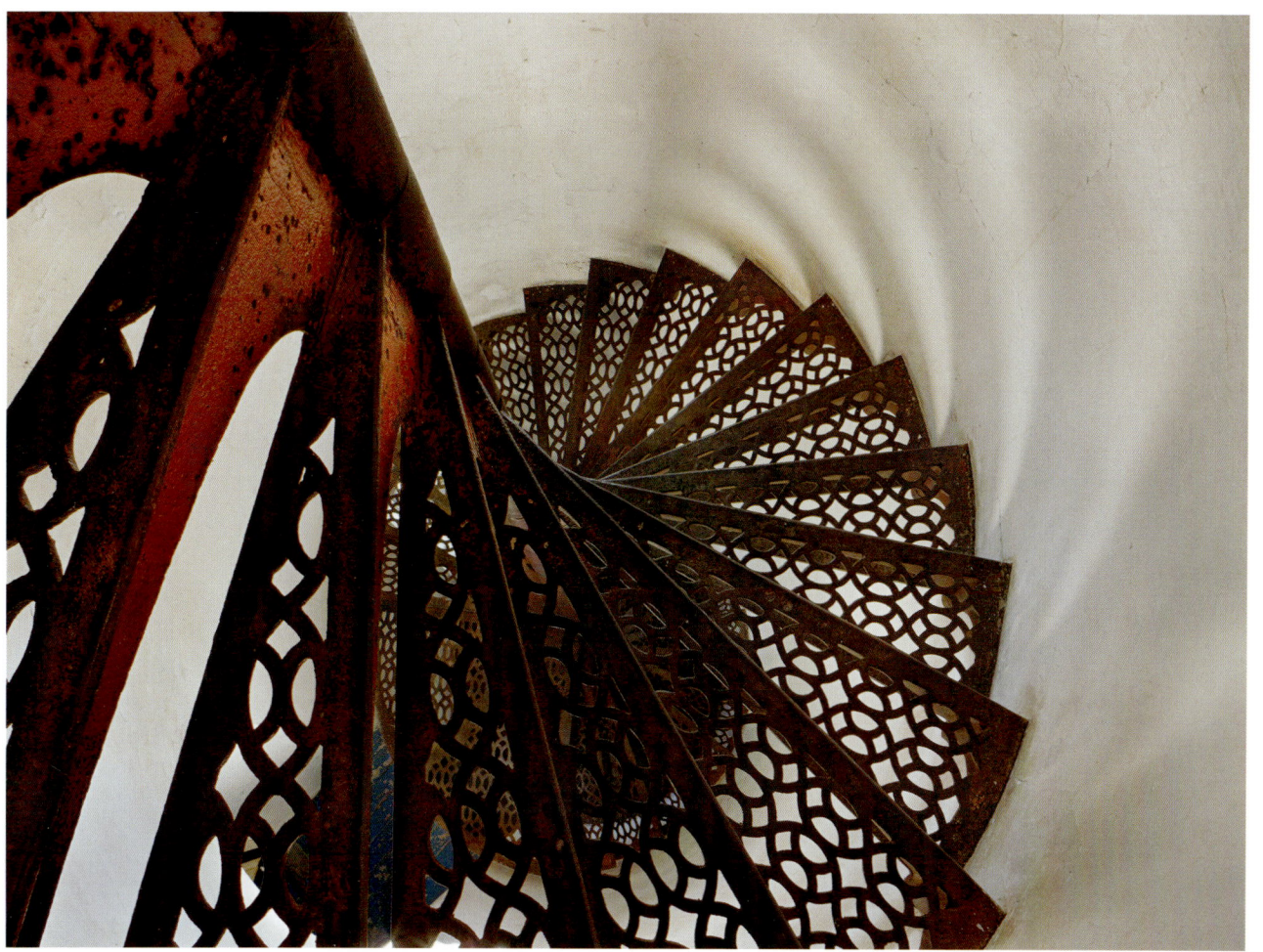

Spiral staircase, Sand Island Lighthouse, Apostle Islands National Lakeshore

Plate 5

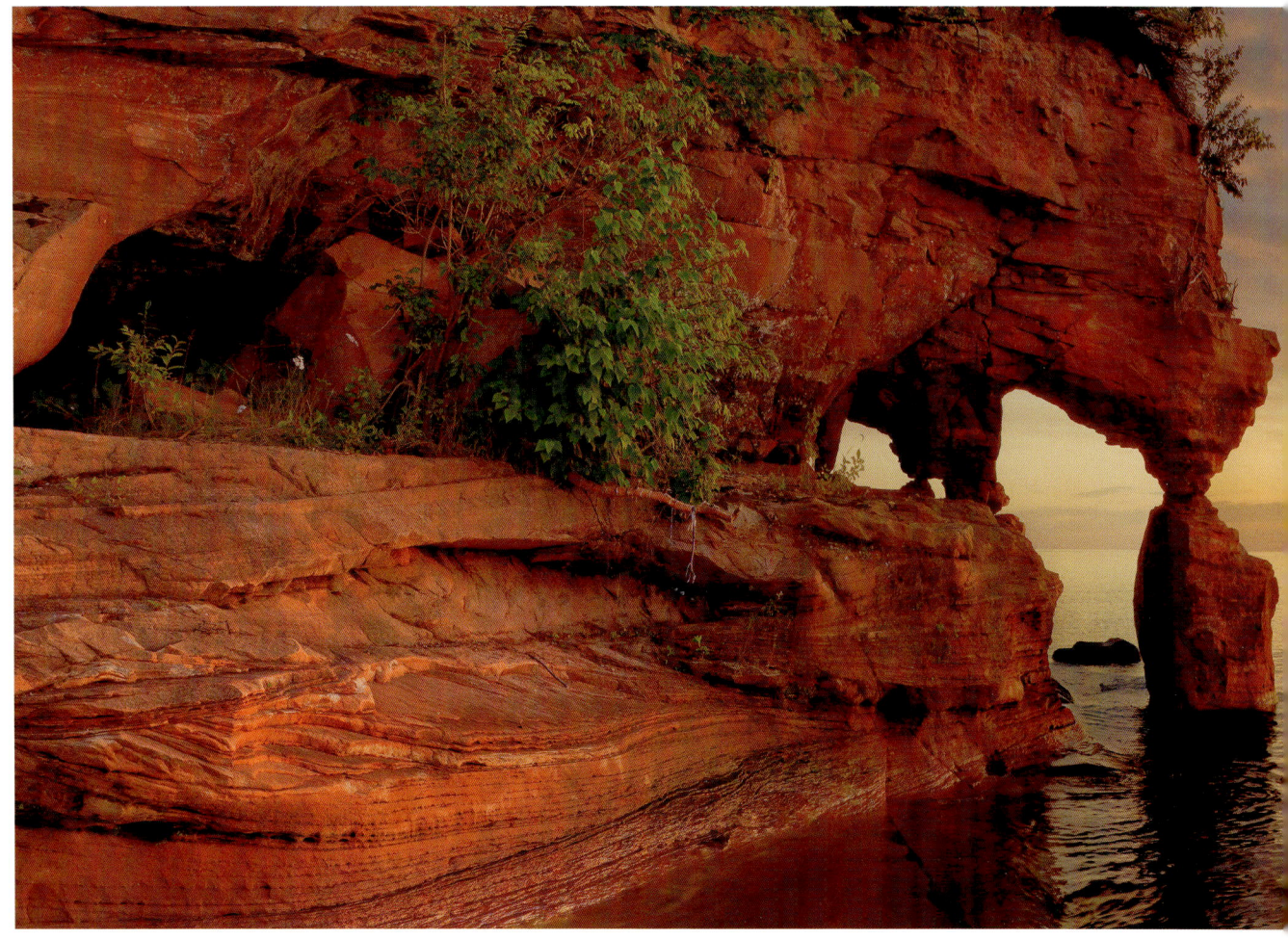

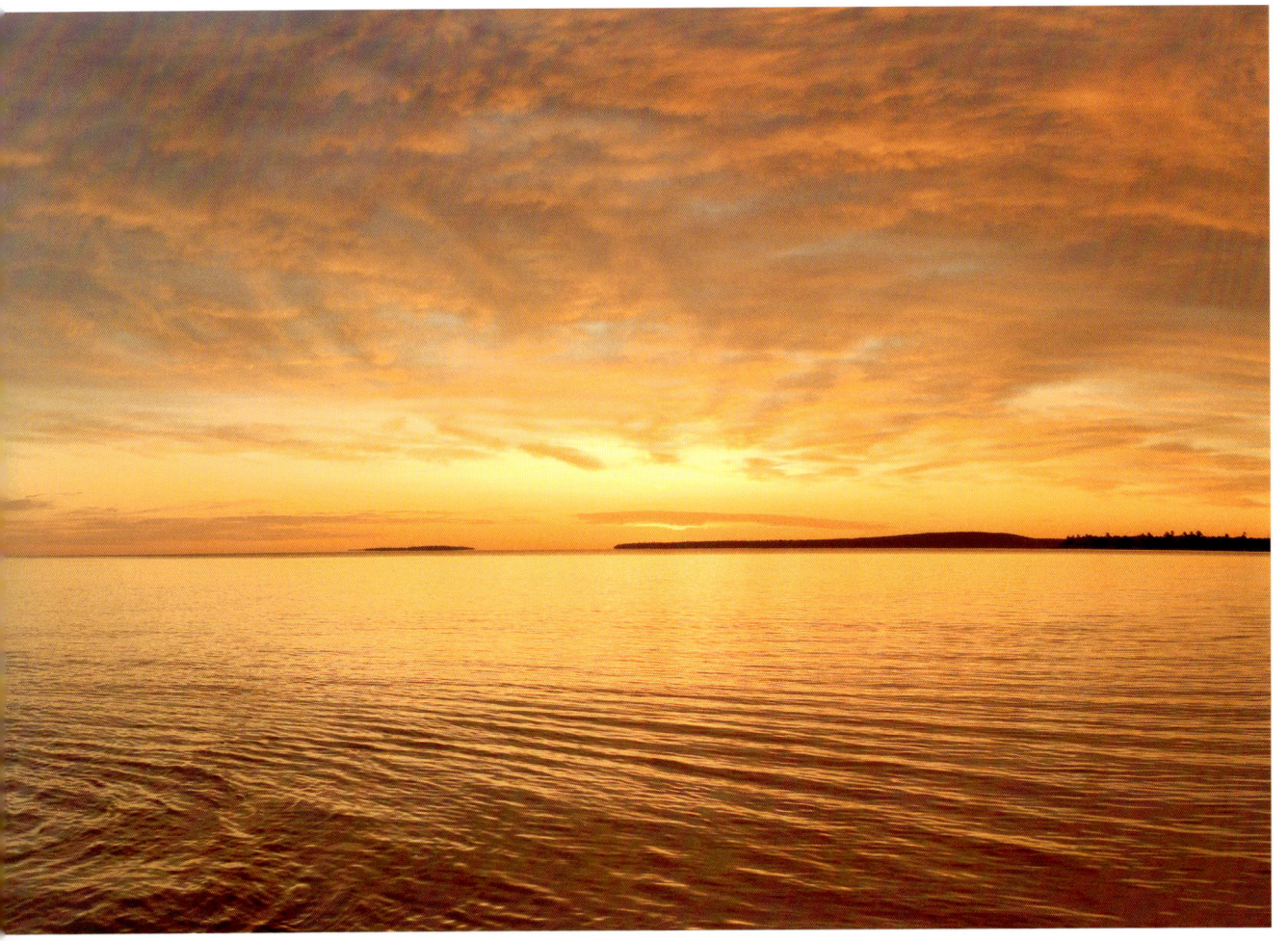

Swallow Point, Sand Island, Apostle Islands National Lakeshore

Plate 6

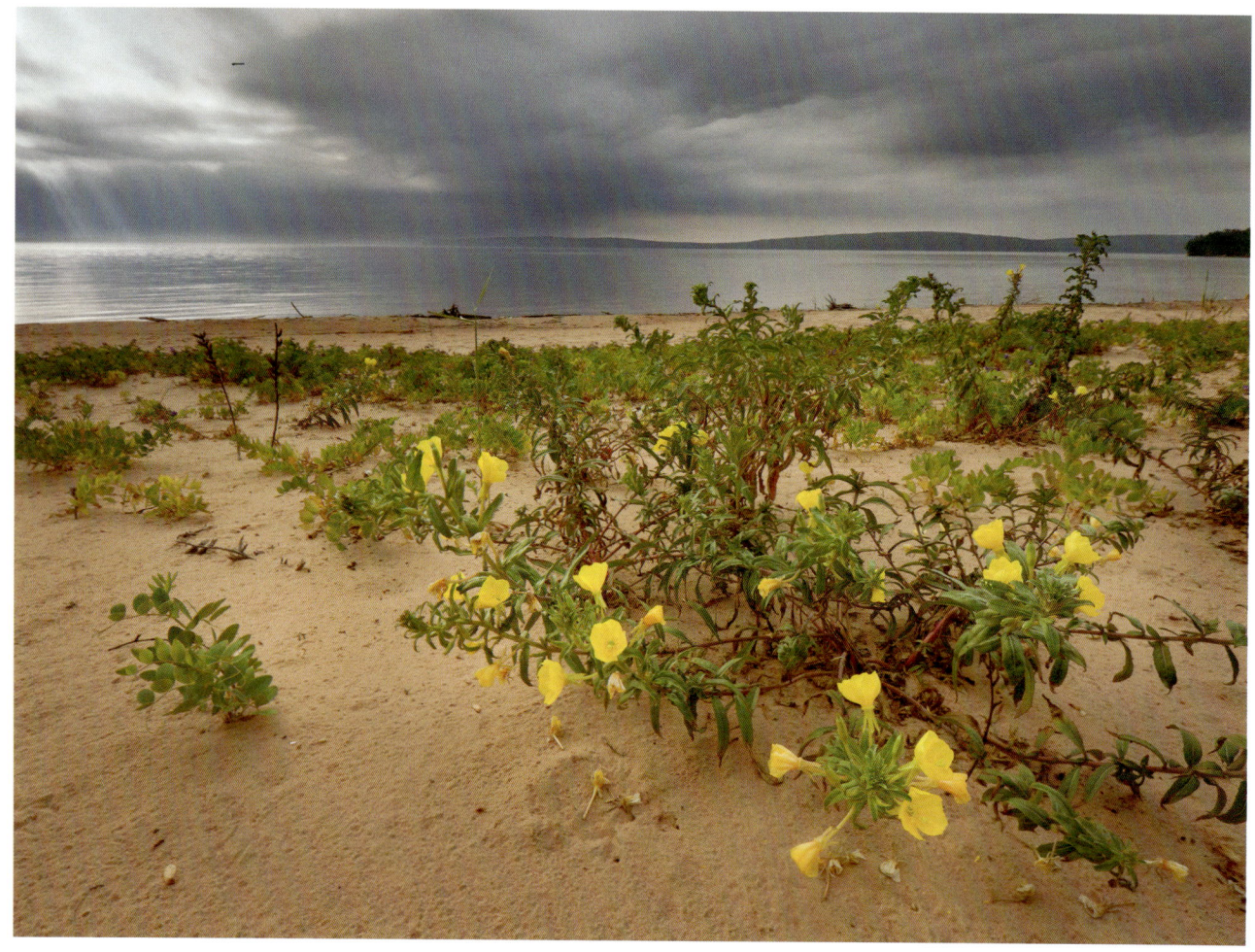

Evening primrose flowers, Sand Island, Apostle Islands National Lakeshore

Plate 7

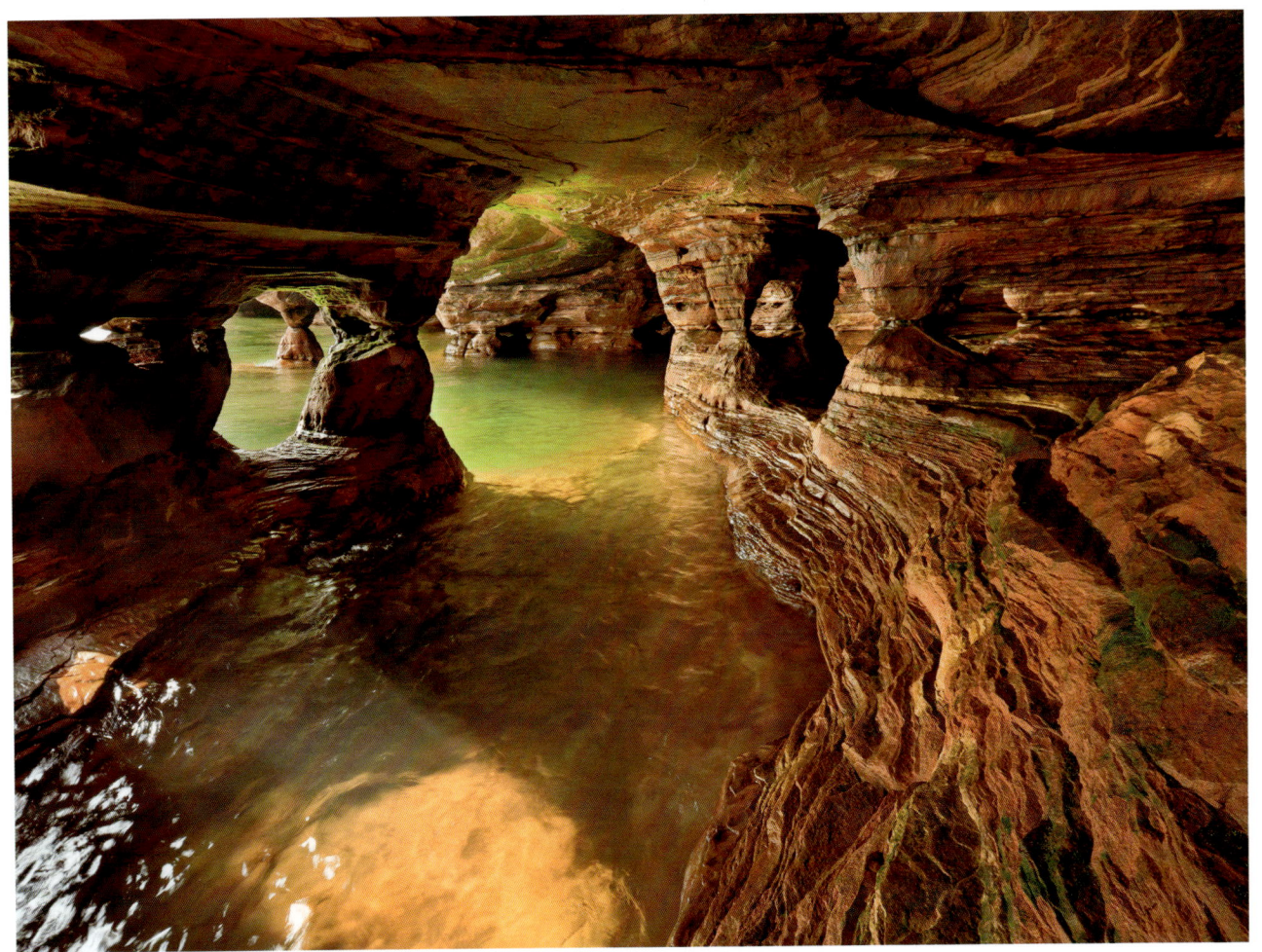

Swallow Point, Sand Island, Apostle Islands National Lakeshore

Plate 8

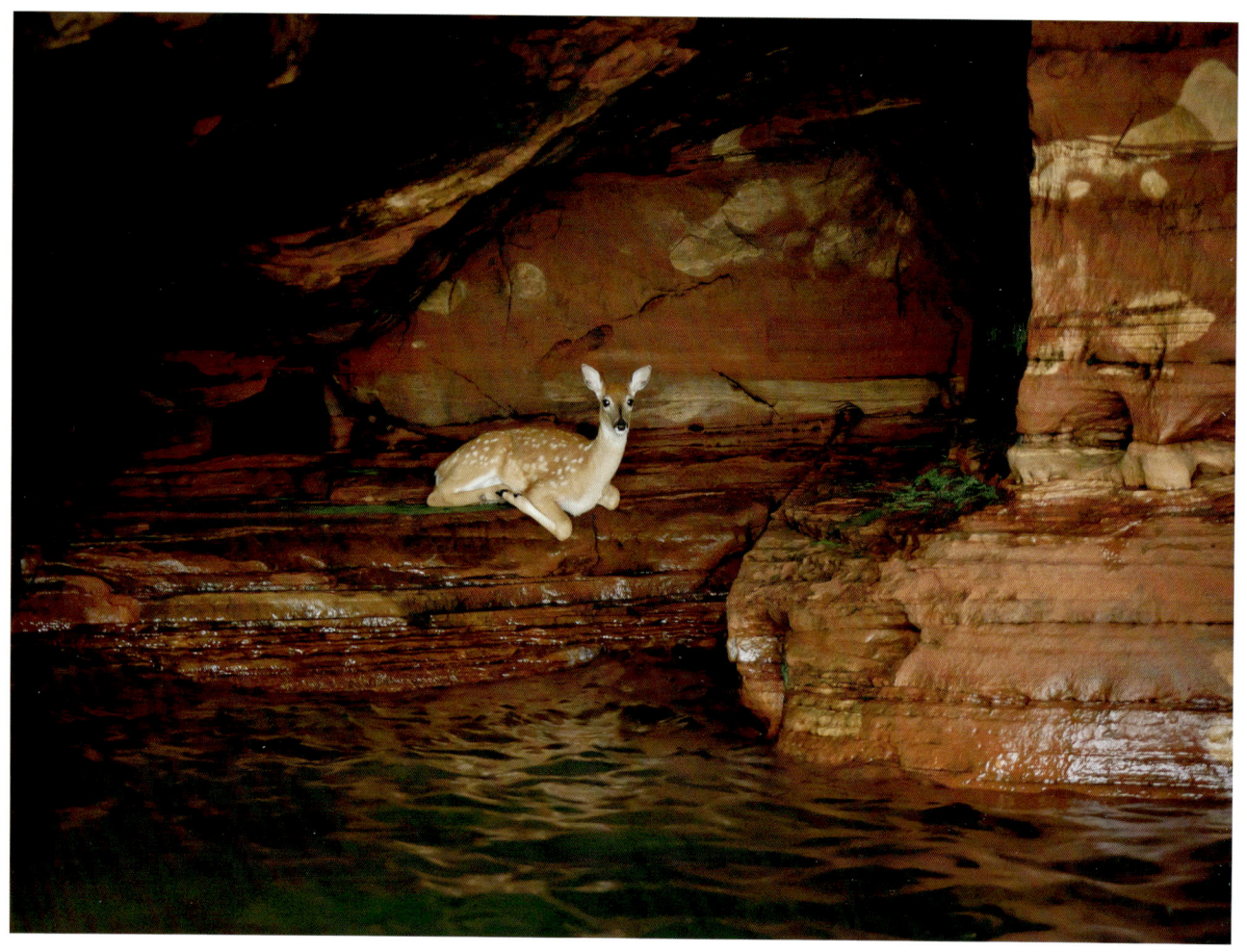

White-tailed deer fawn, Swallow Point, Sand Island, Apostle Islands National Lakeshore

Plate 9

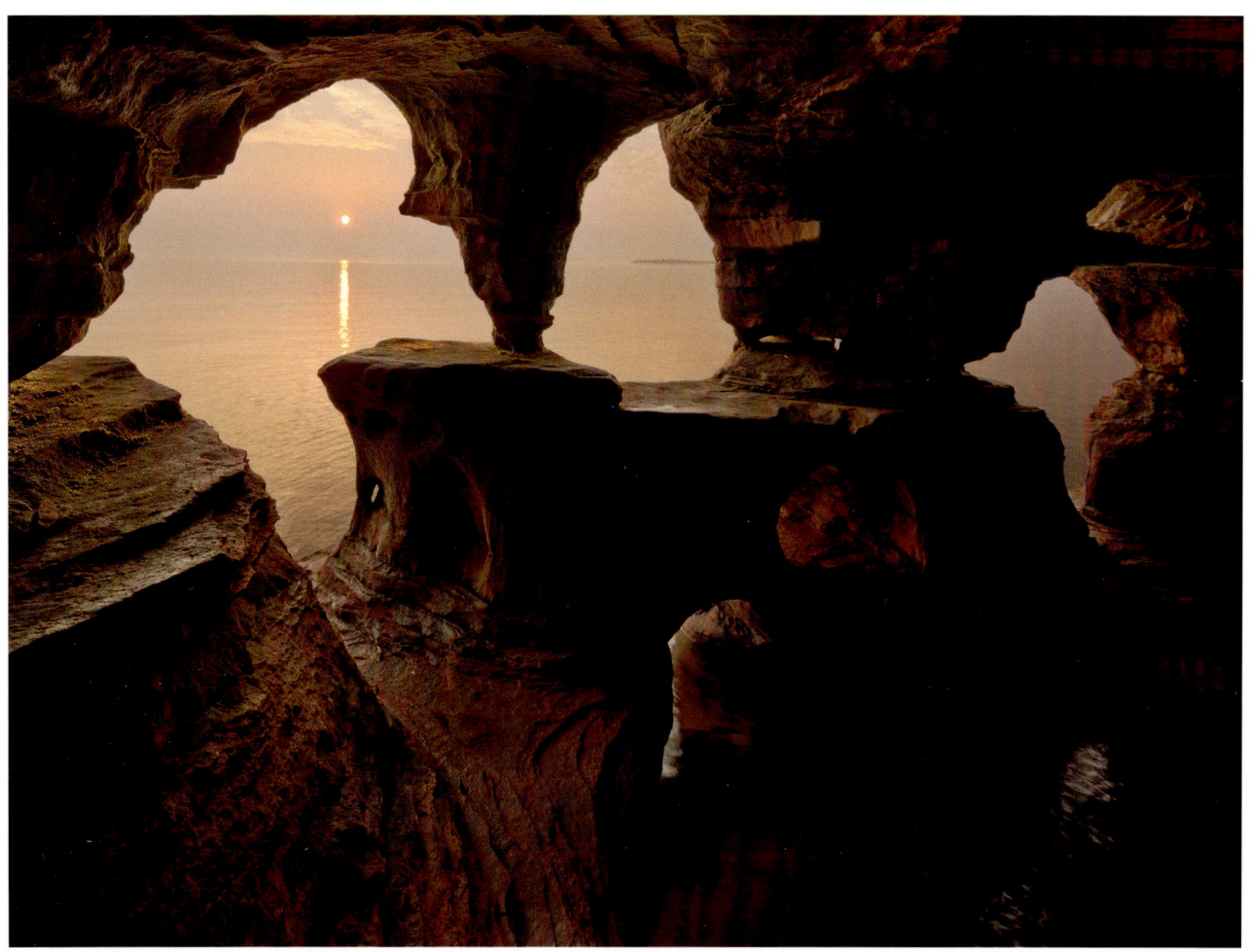

Swallow Point, Sand Island, Apostle Islands National Lakeshore

Plate 10

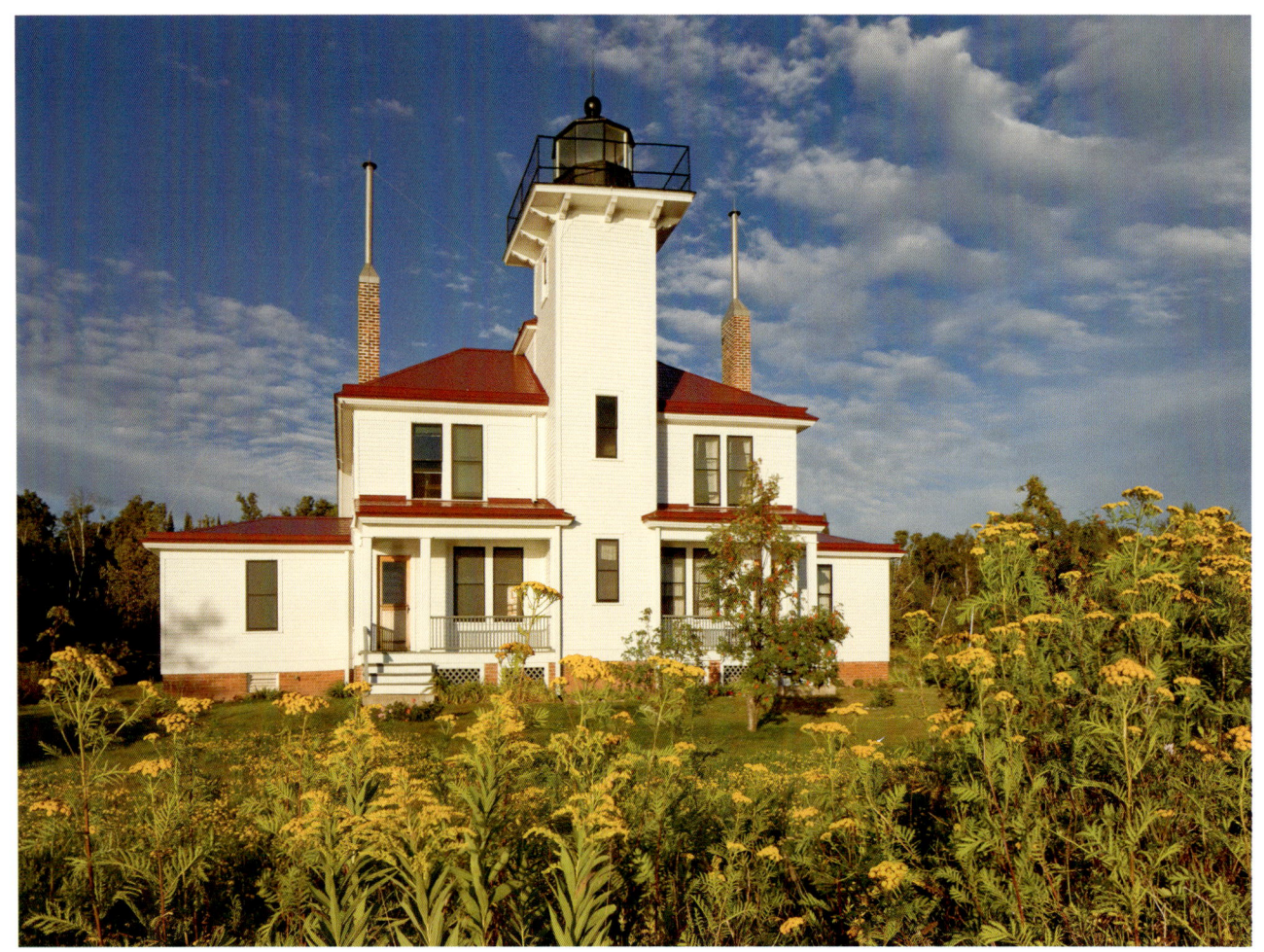

Raspberry Island Lighthouse, Apostle Islands National Lakeshore

Plate 11

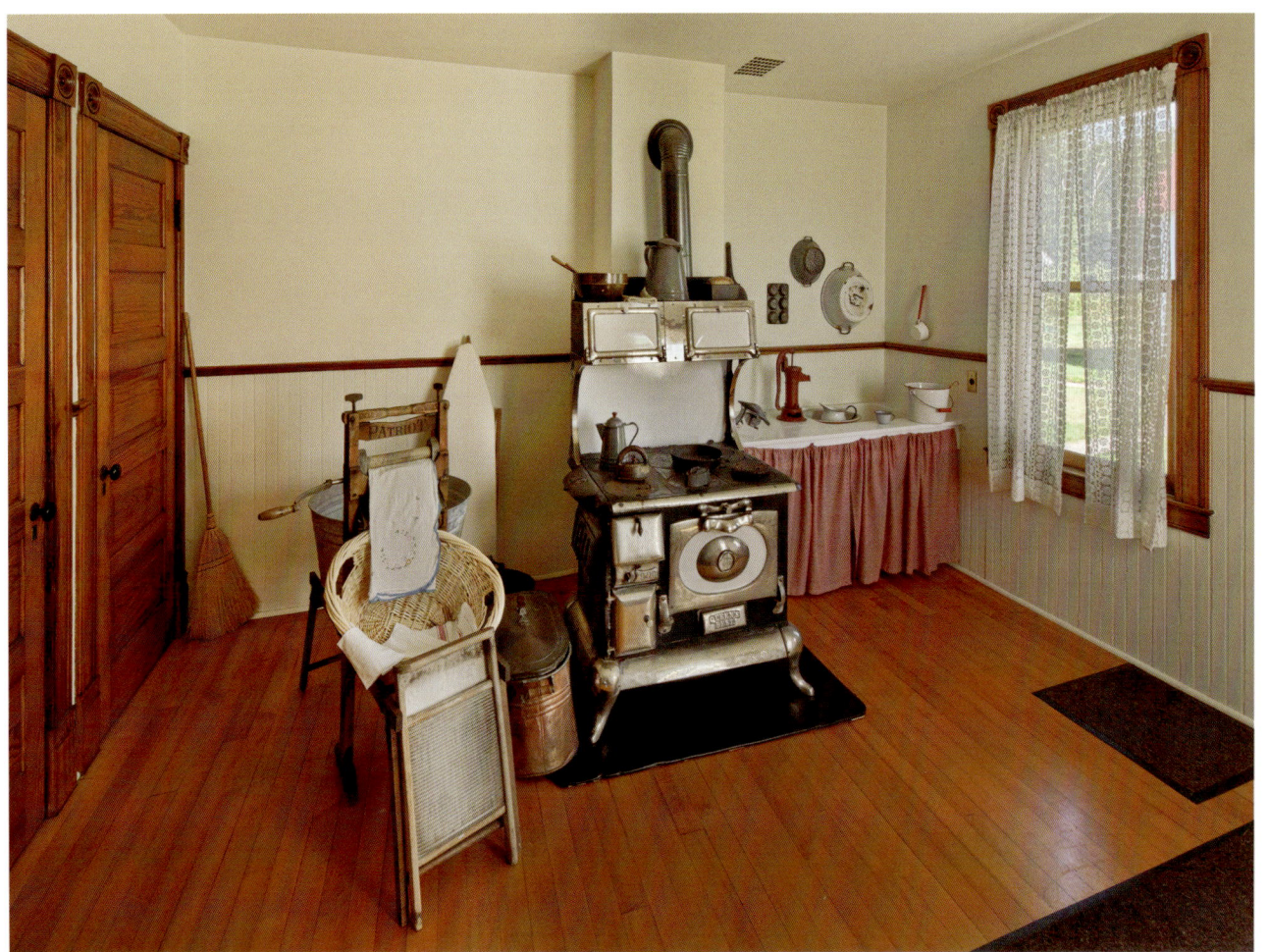

Raspberry Island Lighthouse, Apostle Islands National Lakeshore

Plate 12

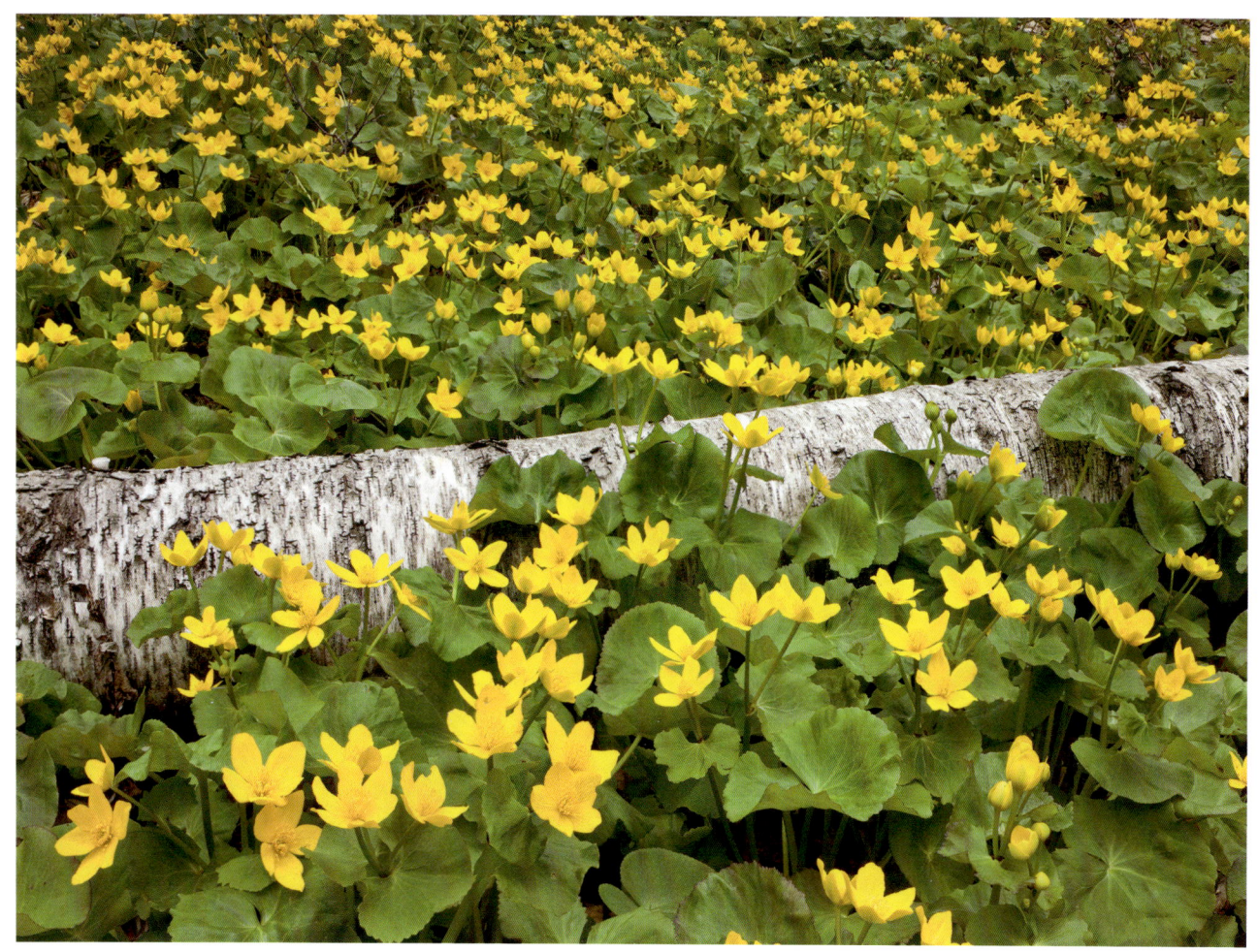

Marsh marigolds and birch log, Oak Island, Apostle Islands National Lakeshore

Plate 13

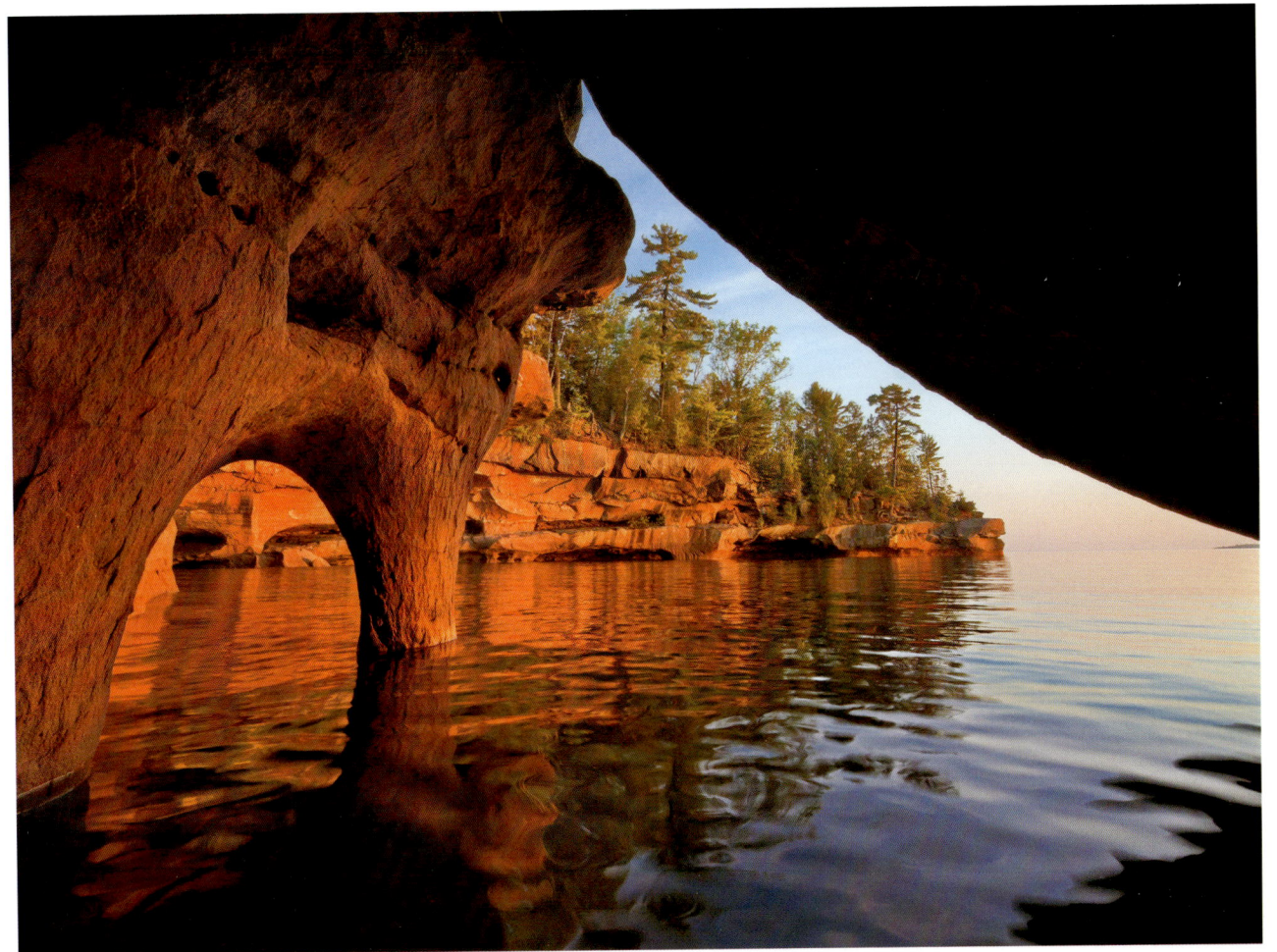

Bear Island, Apostle Islands National Lakeshore

Plate 14

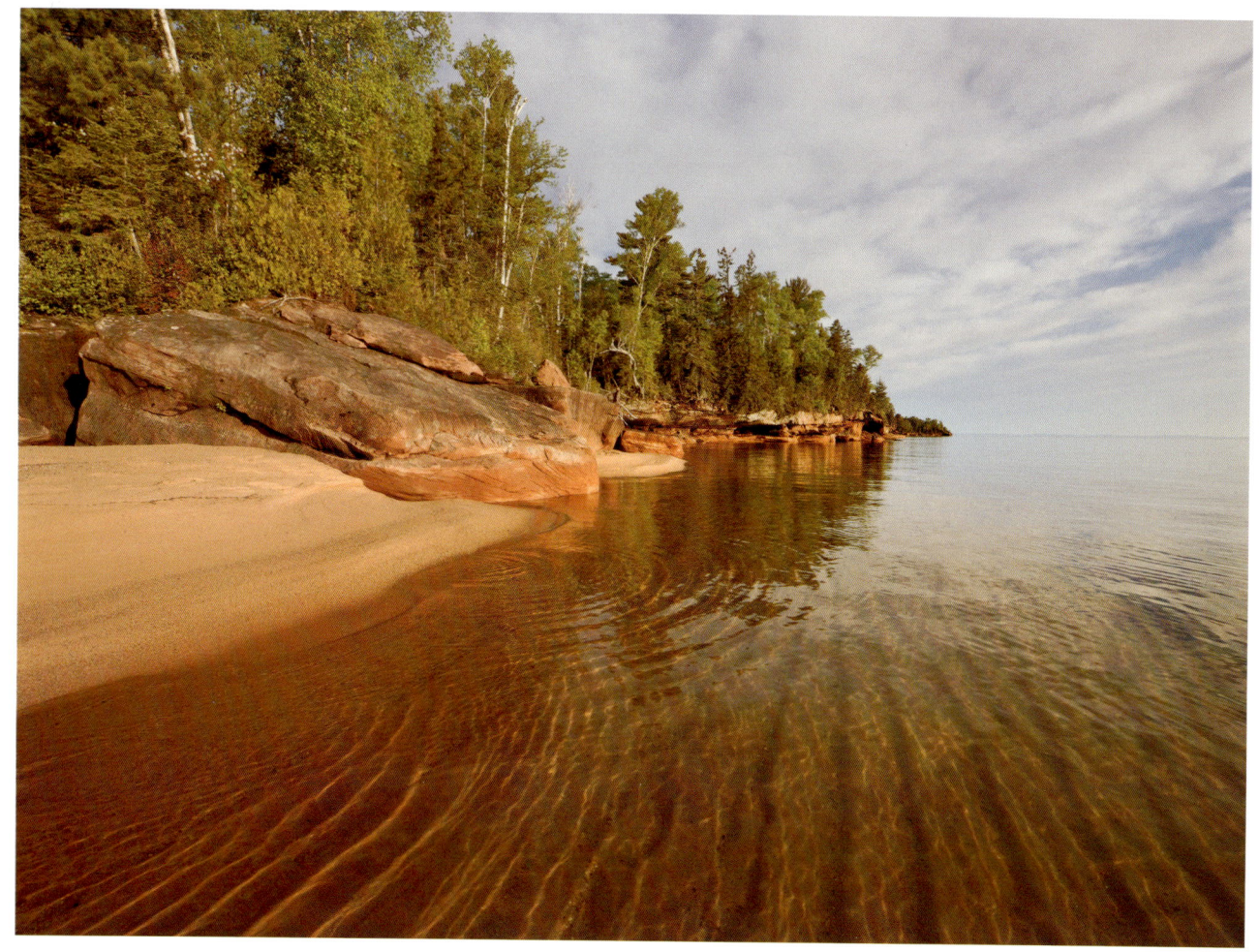

Bear Island, Apostle Islands National Lakeshore

Plate 15

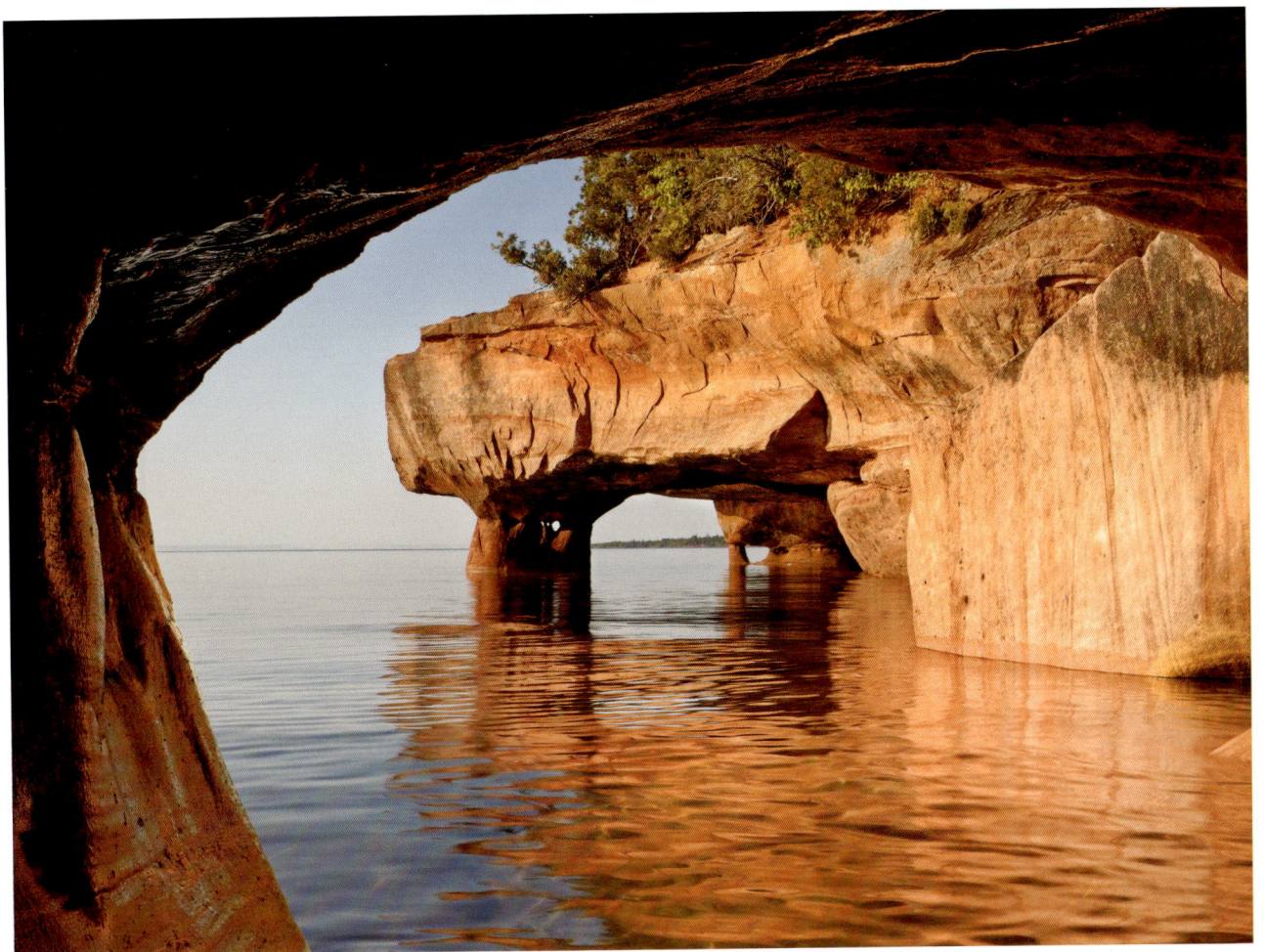

Bear Island, Apostle Islands National Lakeshore

Plate 16

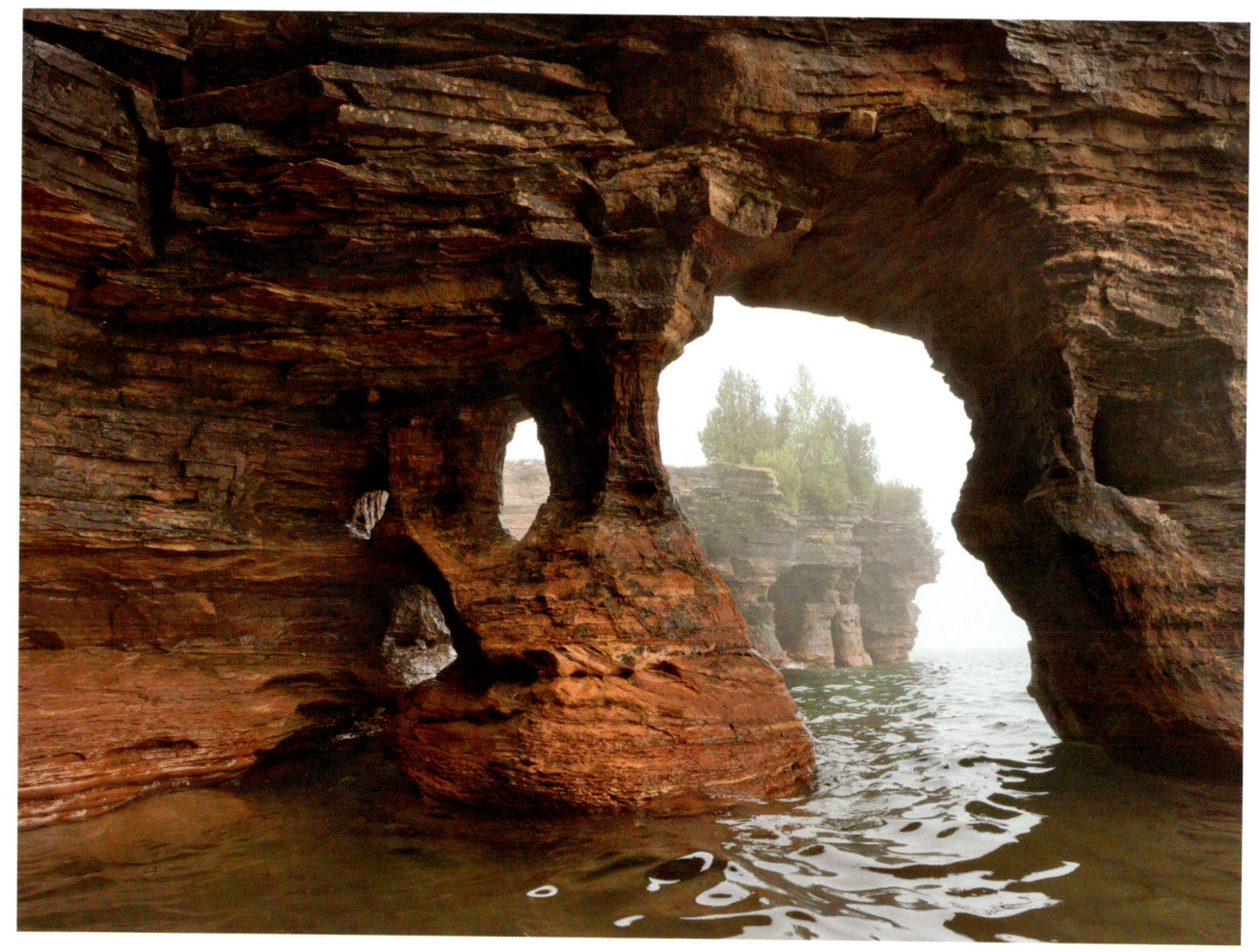

Devils Island, Apostle Islands National Lakeshore

Plate 17

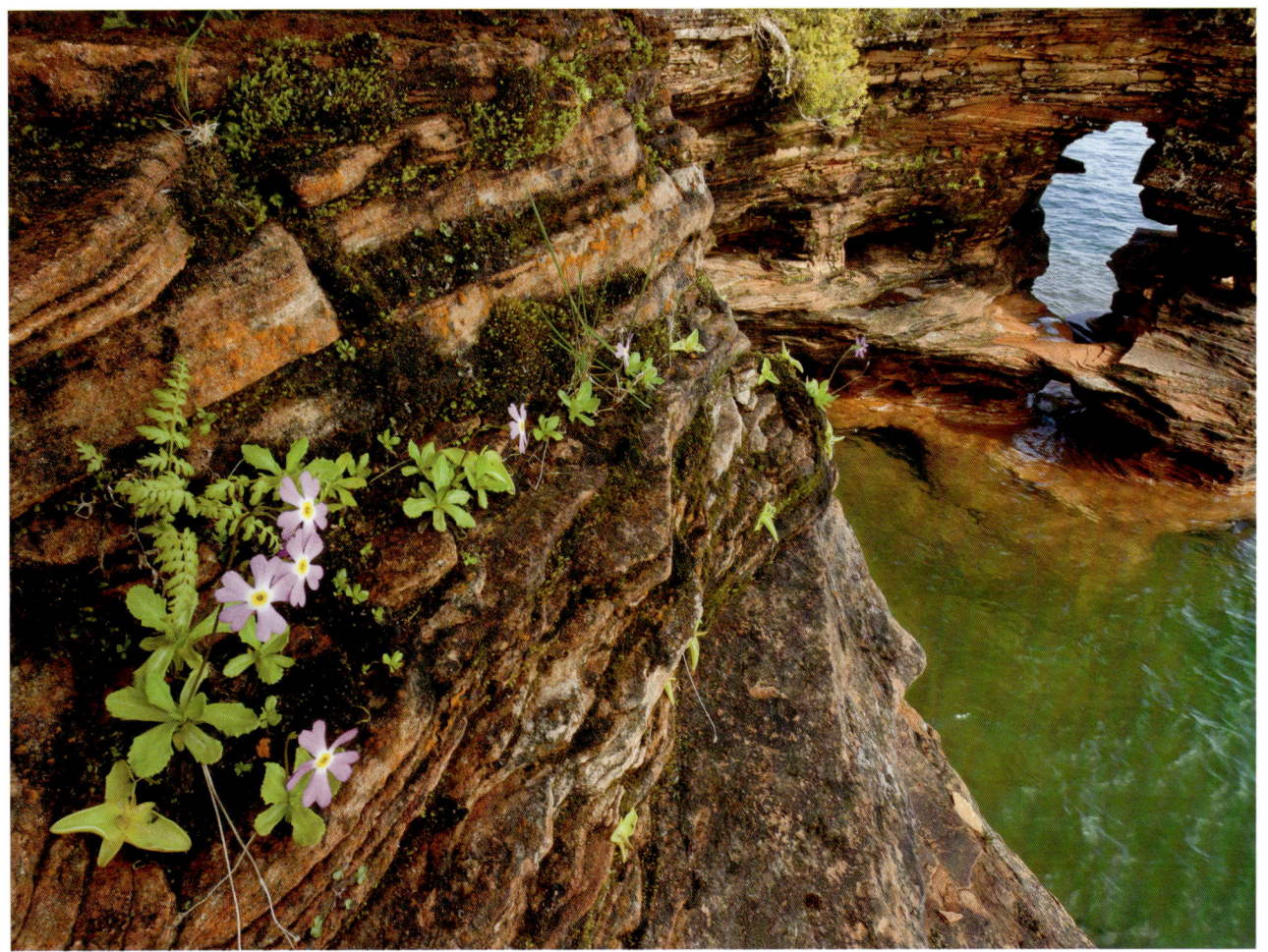

Bird's-eye primrose flowers, Devils Island, Apostle Islands National Lakeshore

Plate 18

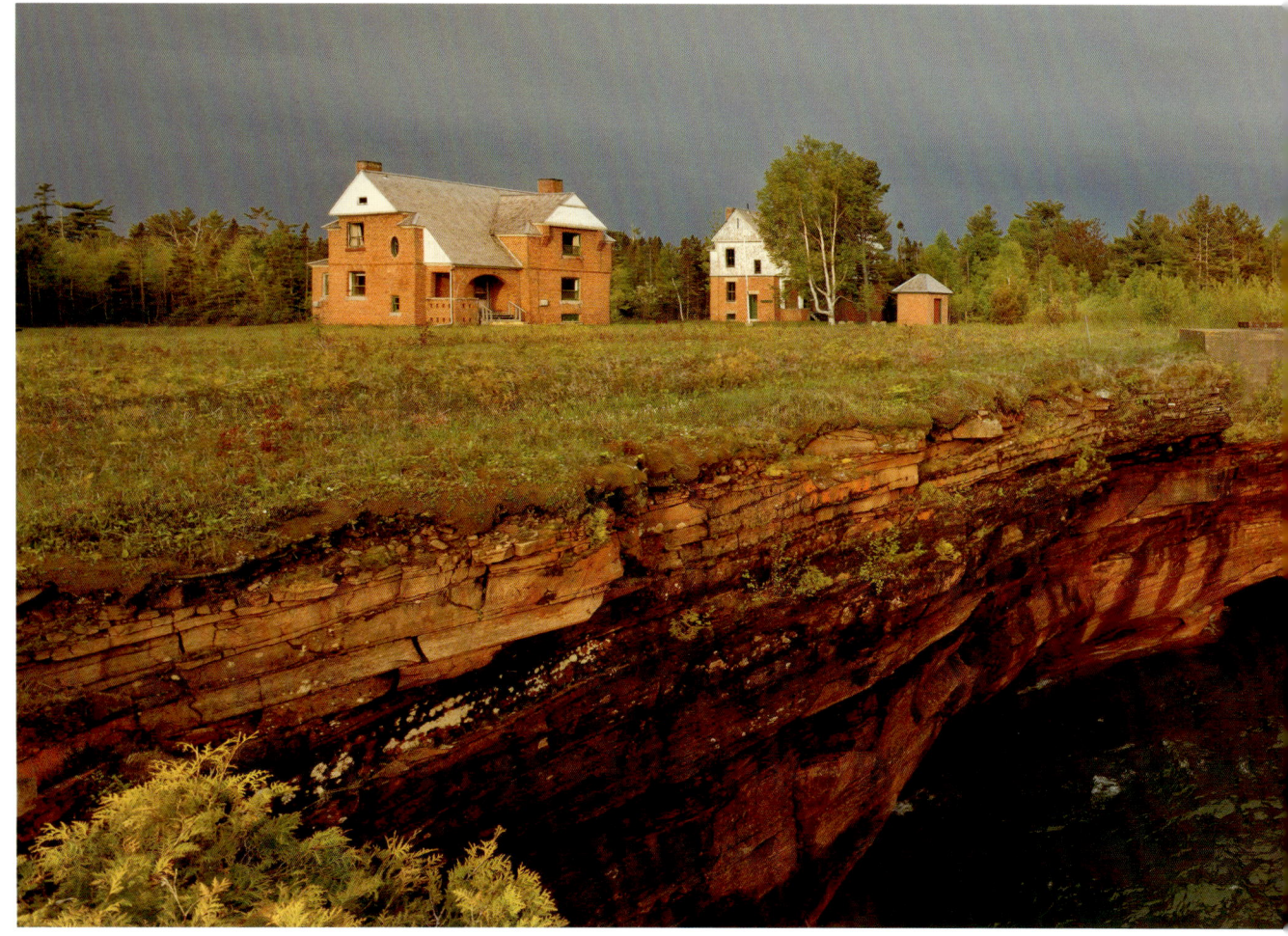

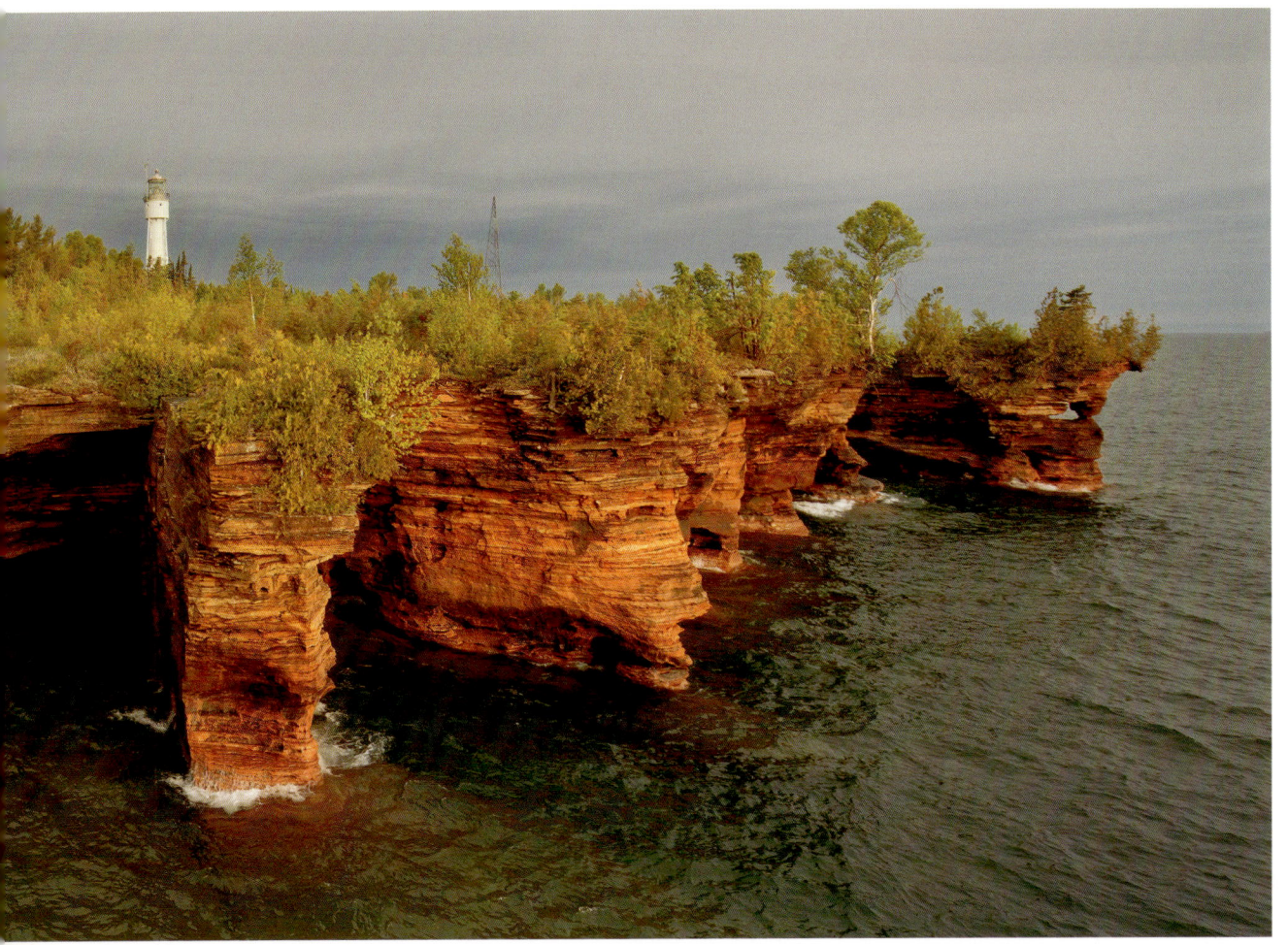

Devils Island Light Station, Apostle Islands National Lakeshore

Plate 19

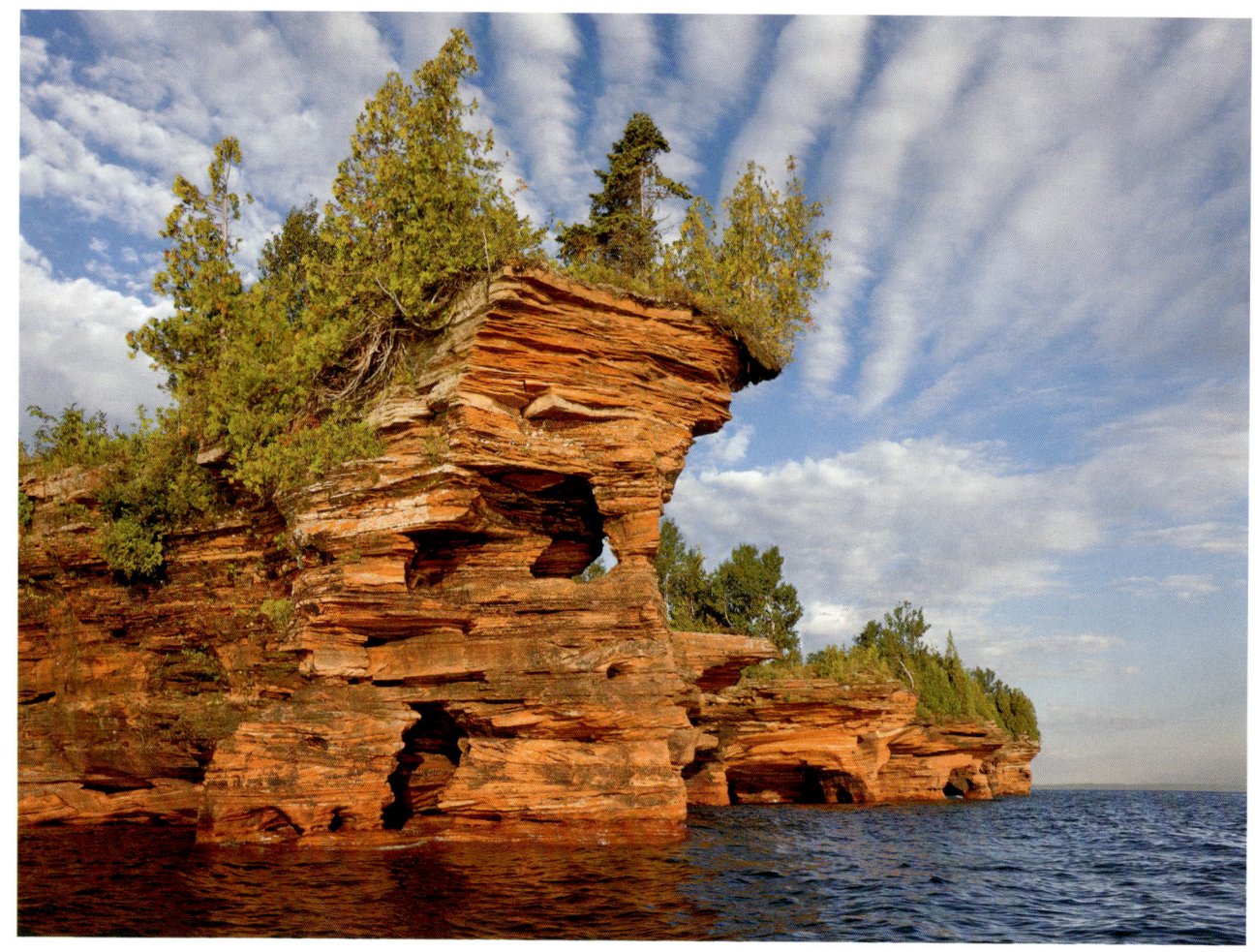

Devils Island, Apostle Islands National Lakeshore

Plate 20

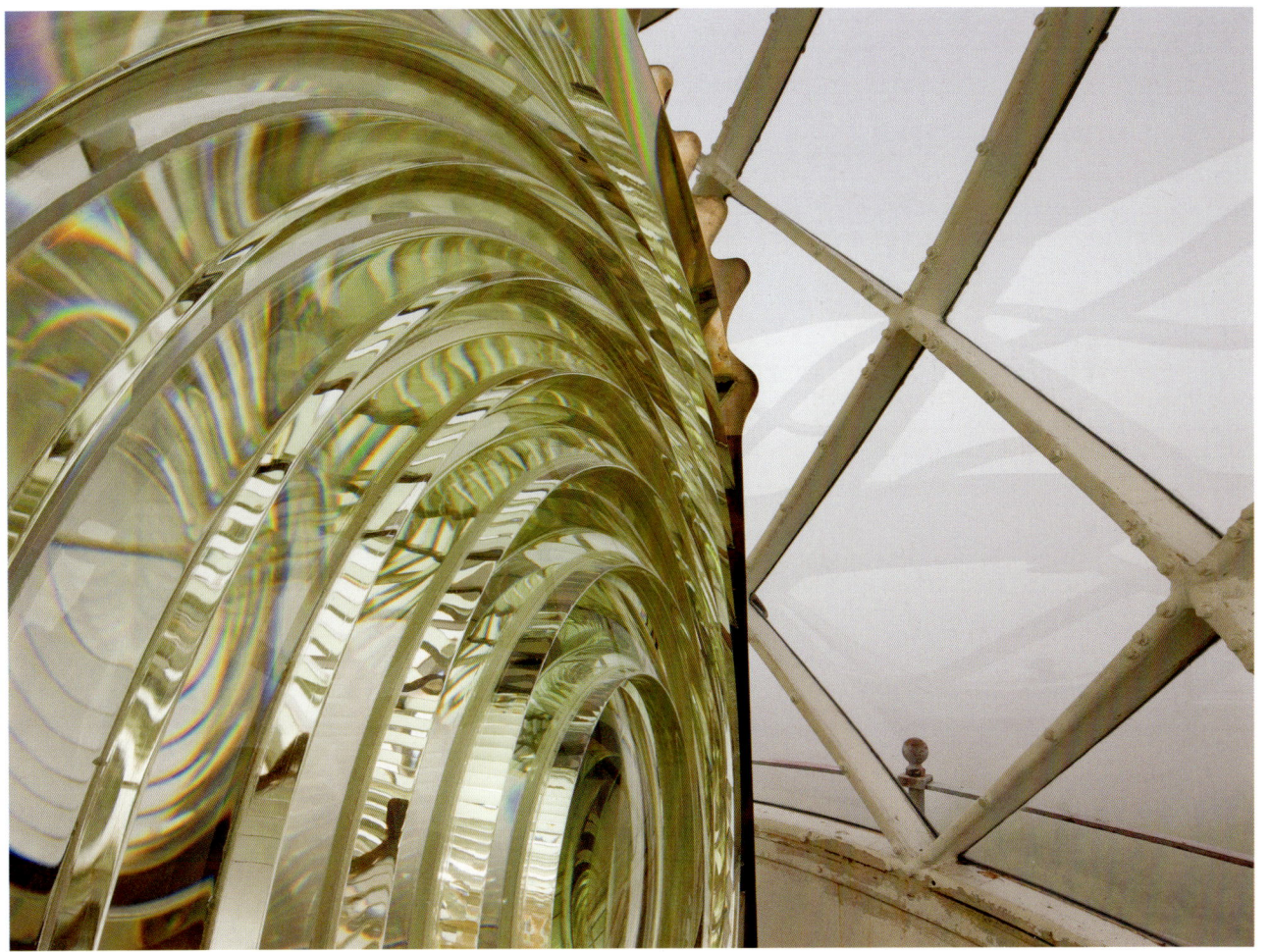

Fresnel lens, Devils Island Light, Apostle Islands National Lakeshore

Plate 21

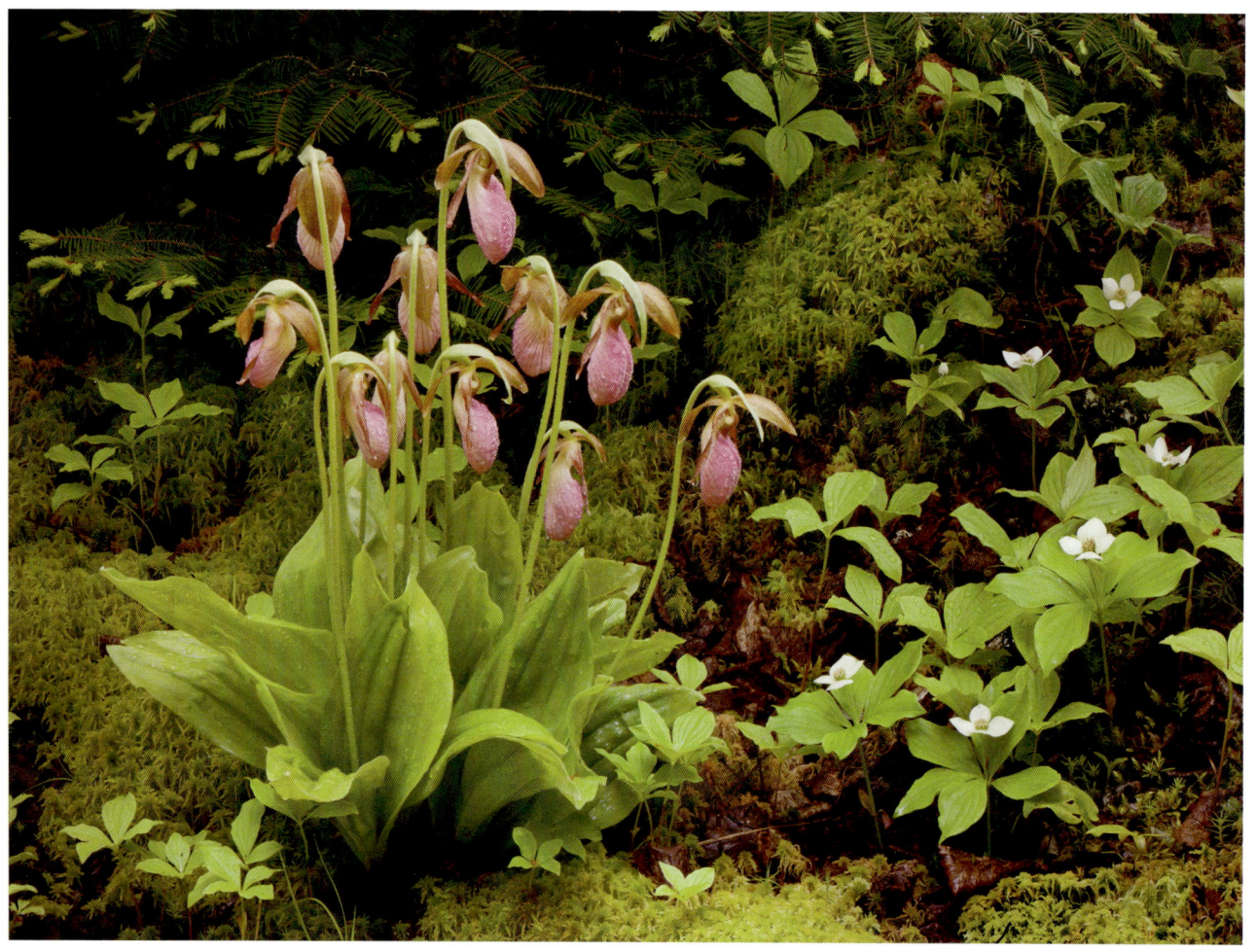

Stemless lady's slippers and bunchberry flowers, Devils Island, Apostle Islands National Lakeshore

Plate 22

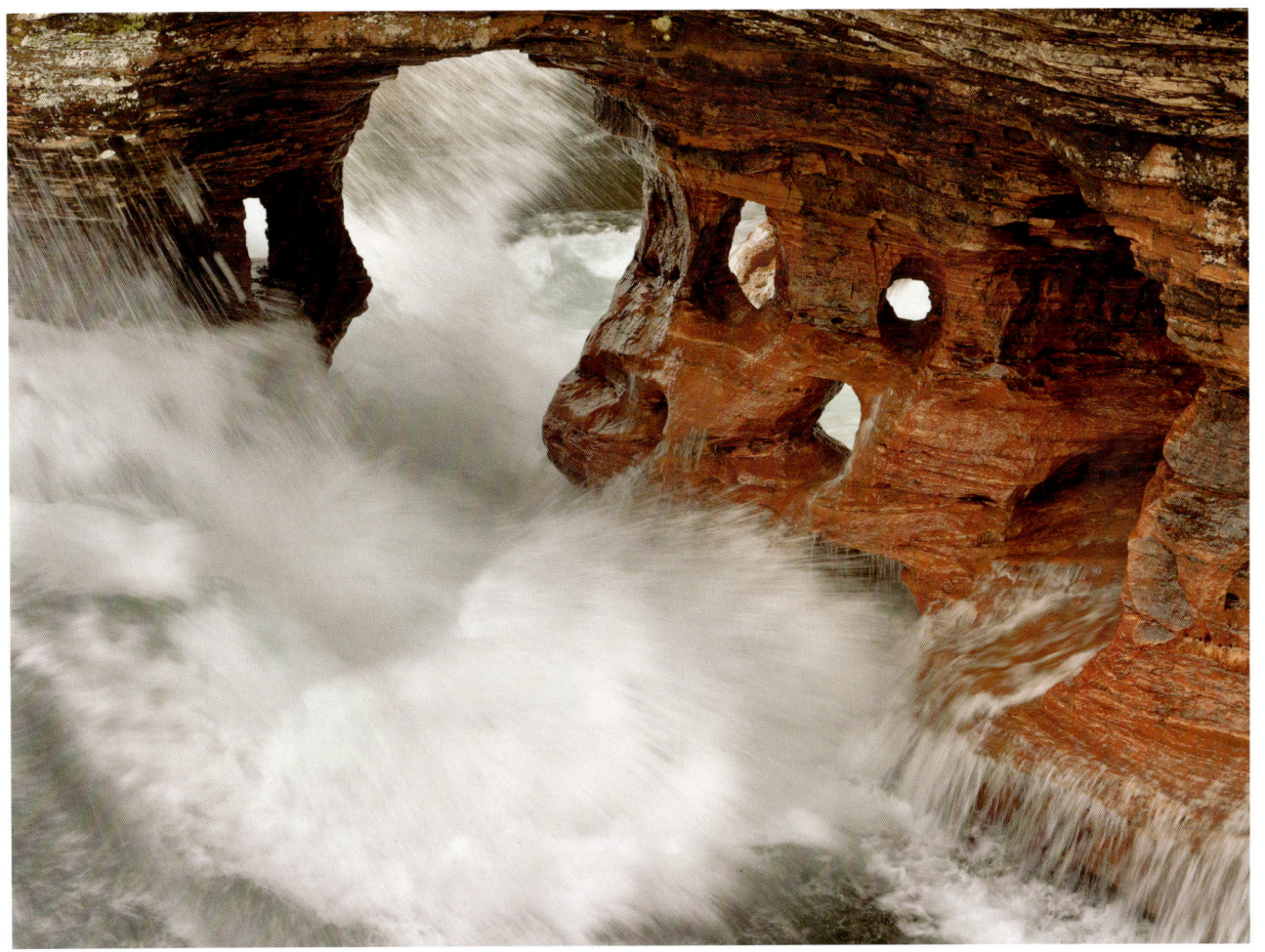

Devils Island, Apostle Islands National Lakeshore

Plate 23

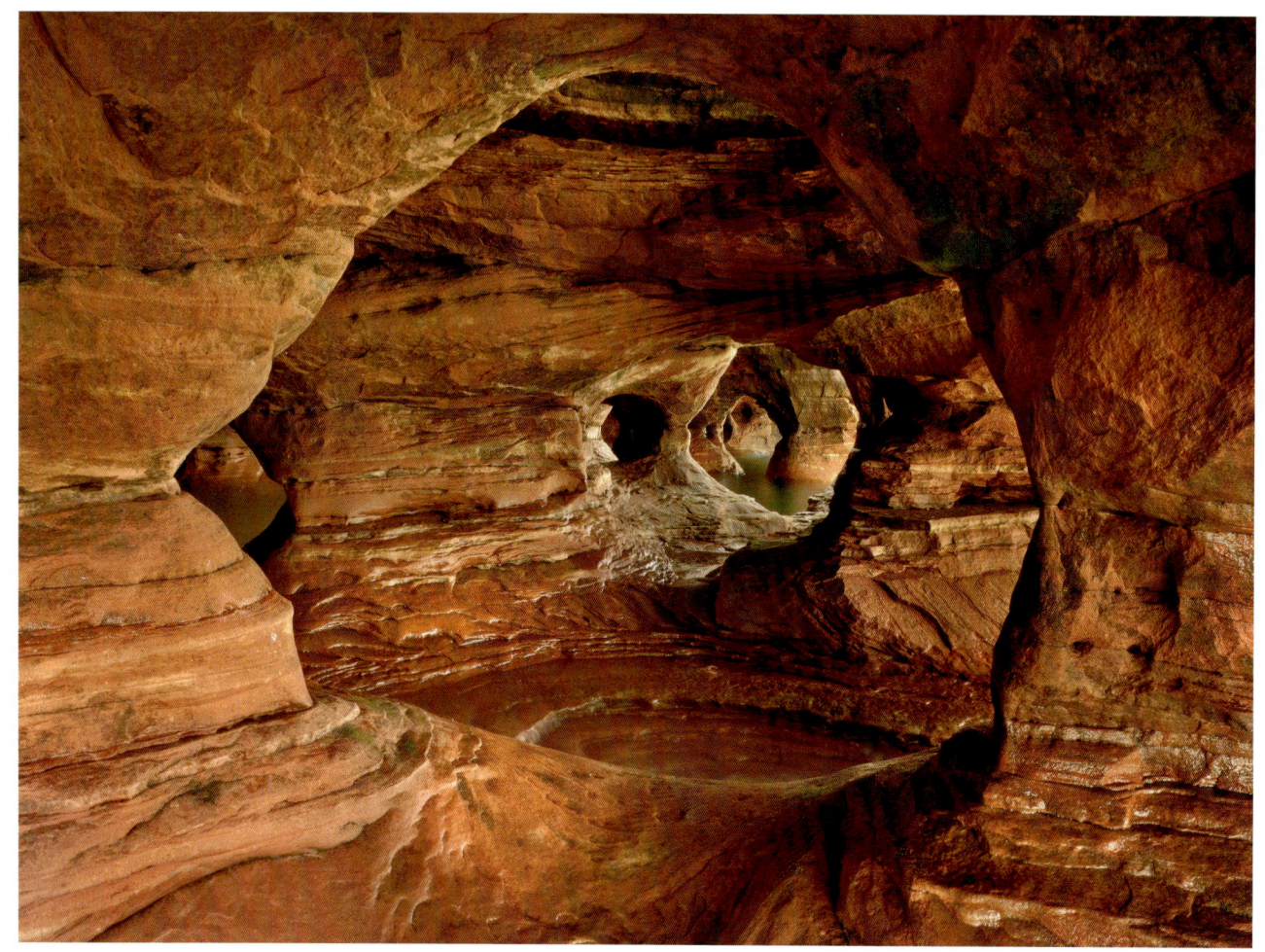

Devils Island, Apostle Islands National Lakeshore

Plate 24

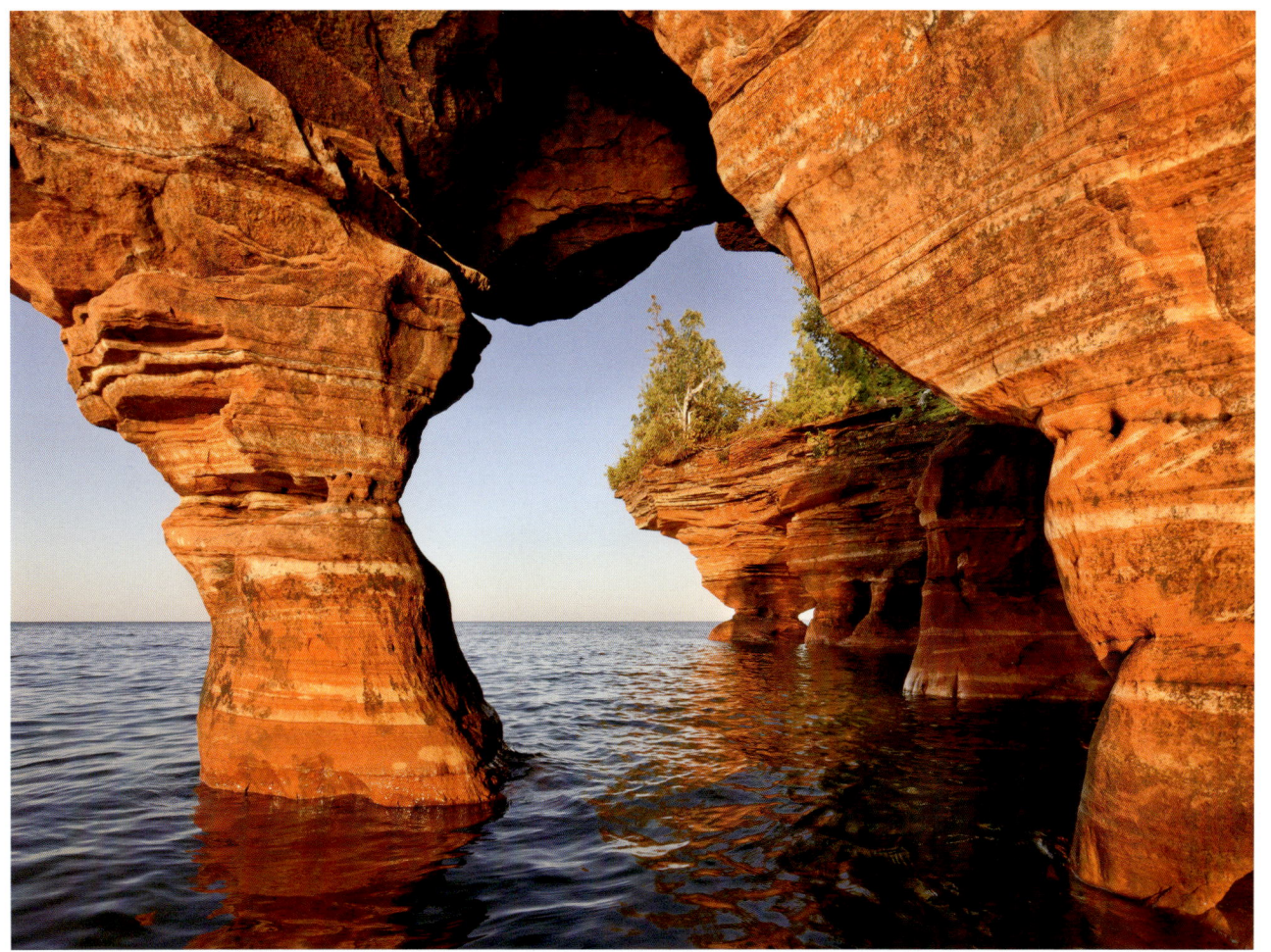

Devils Island, Apostle Islands National Lakeshore

Plate 25

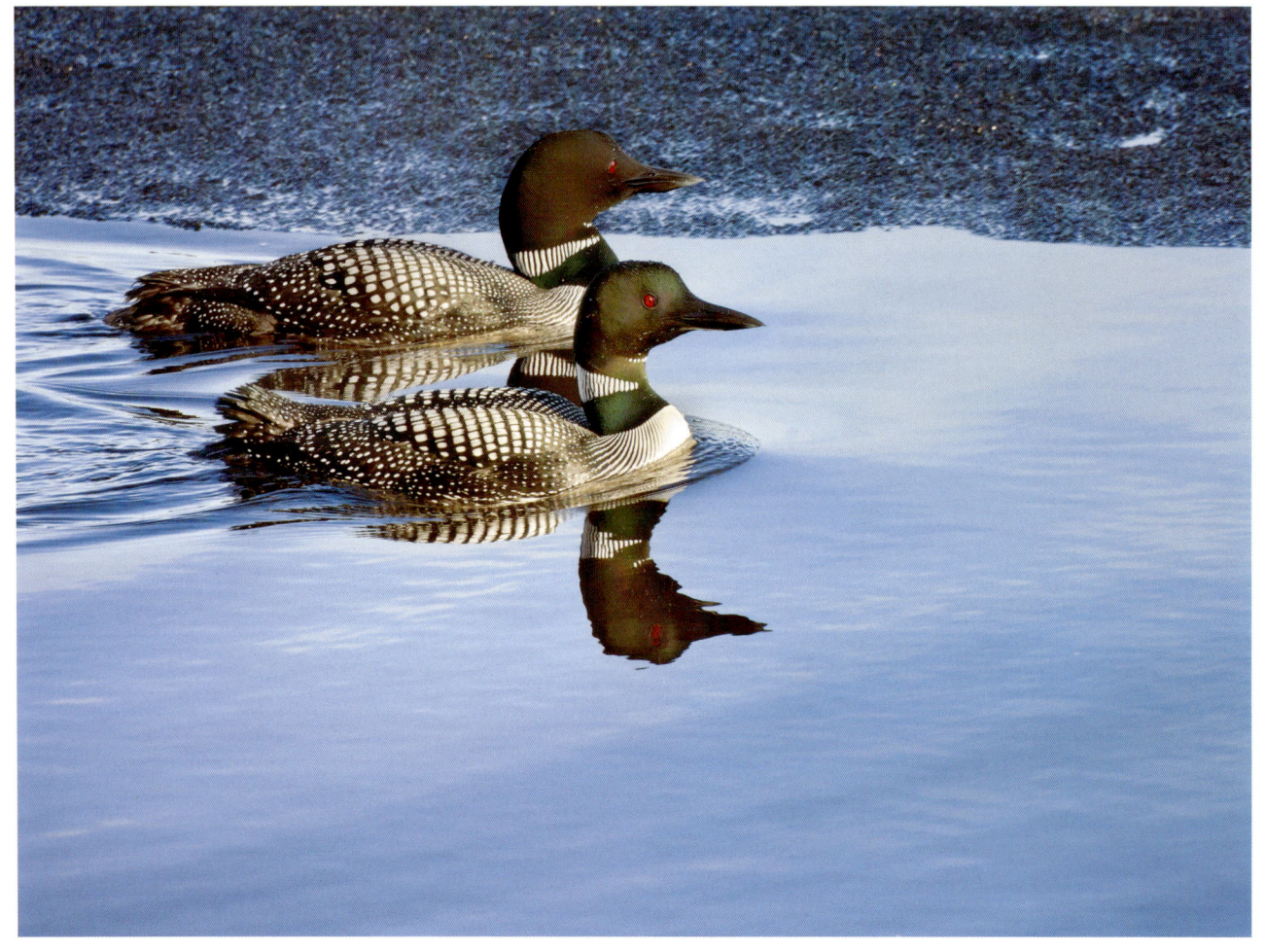

Great northern loons at edge of ice

Plate 26

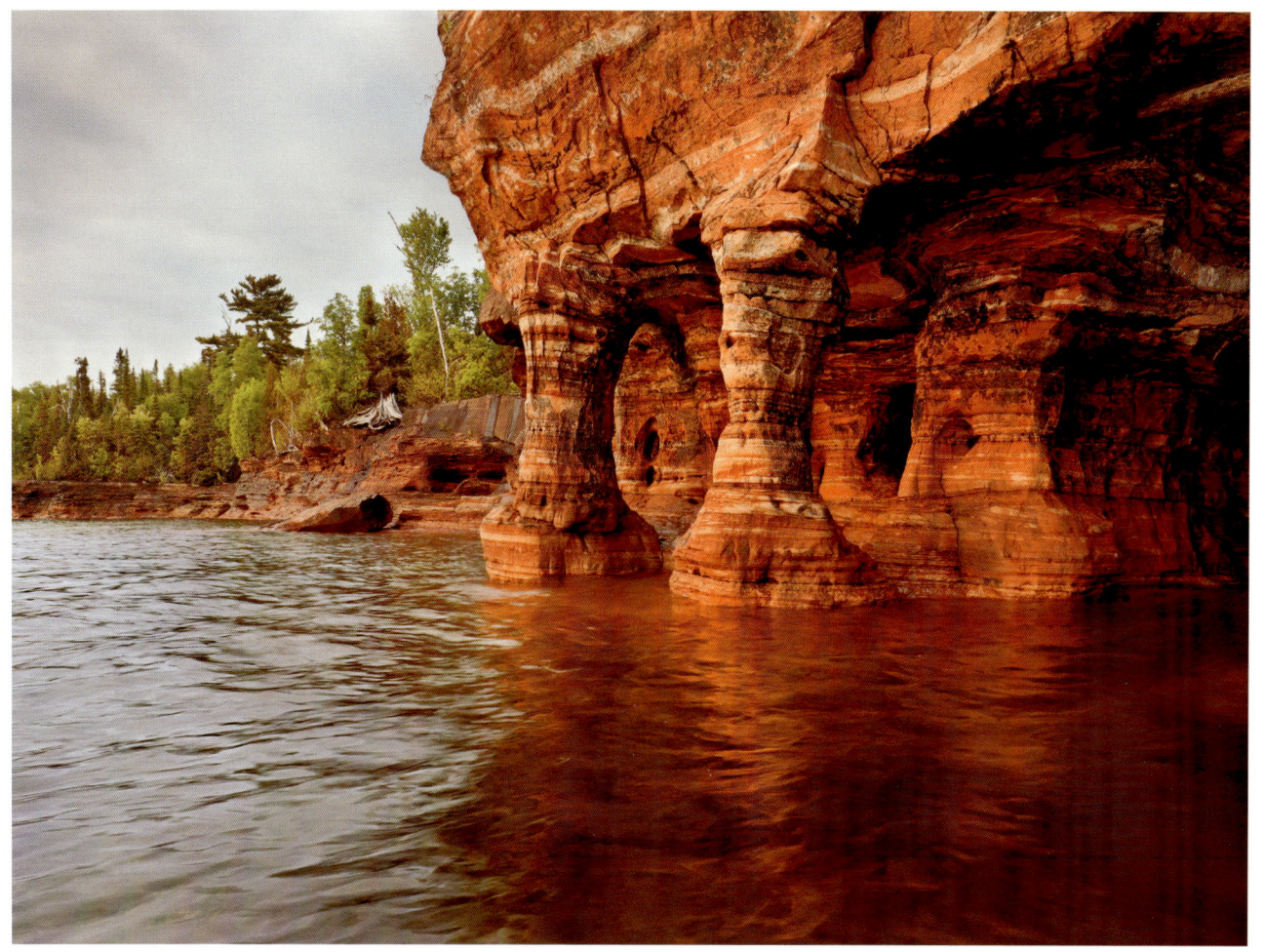

Devils Island, Apostle Islands National Lakeshore

Plate 27

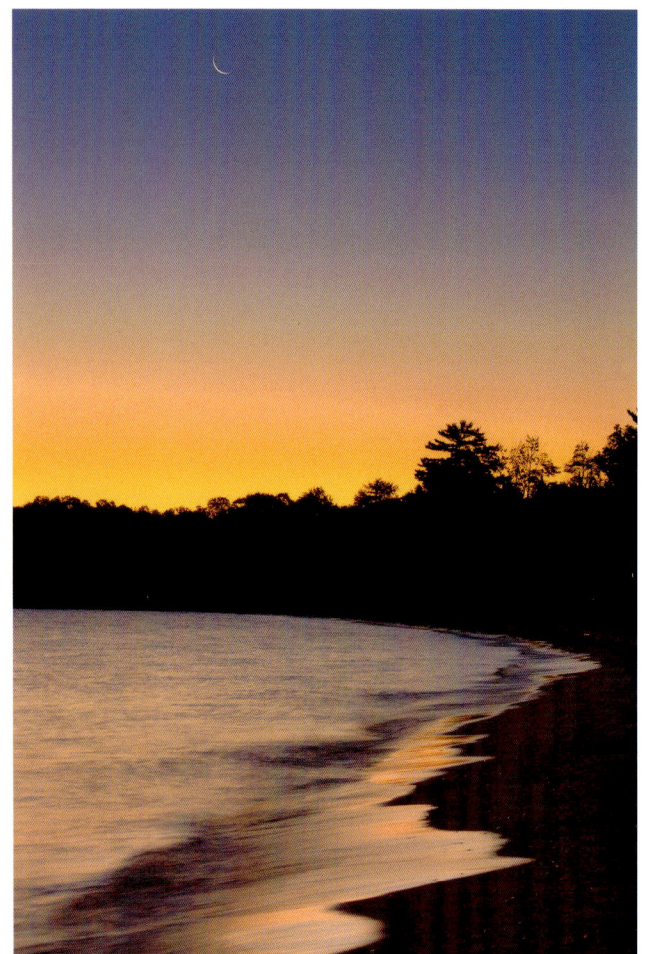

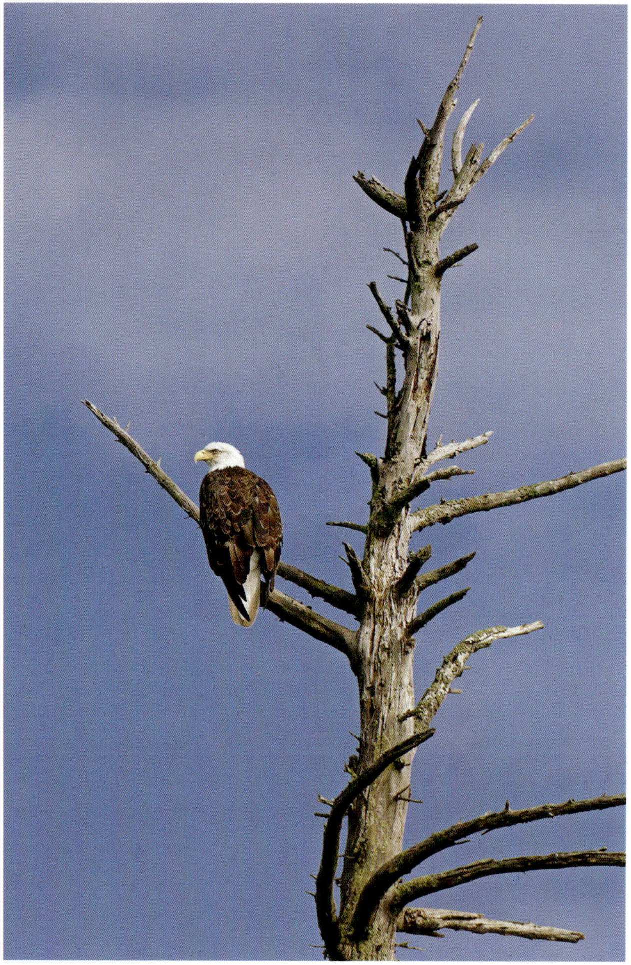

Rocky Island, Apostle Islands National Lakeshore / Bald eagle

Plates 28, 29

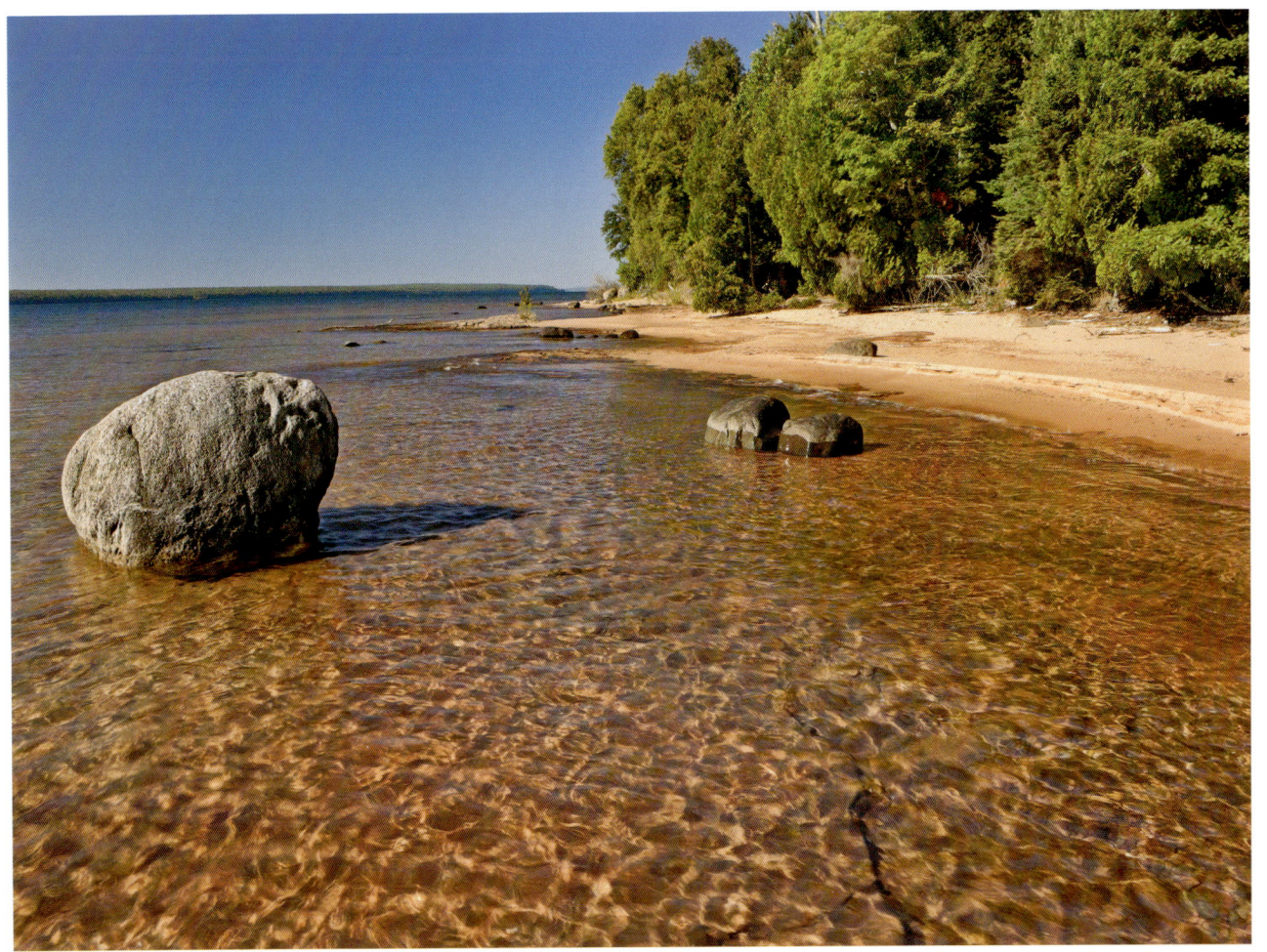

Glacial erratics, Cat Island, Apostle Islands National Lakeshore

Plate 30

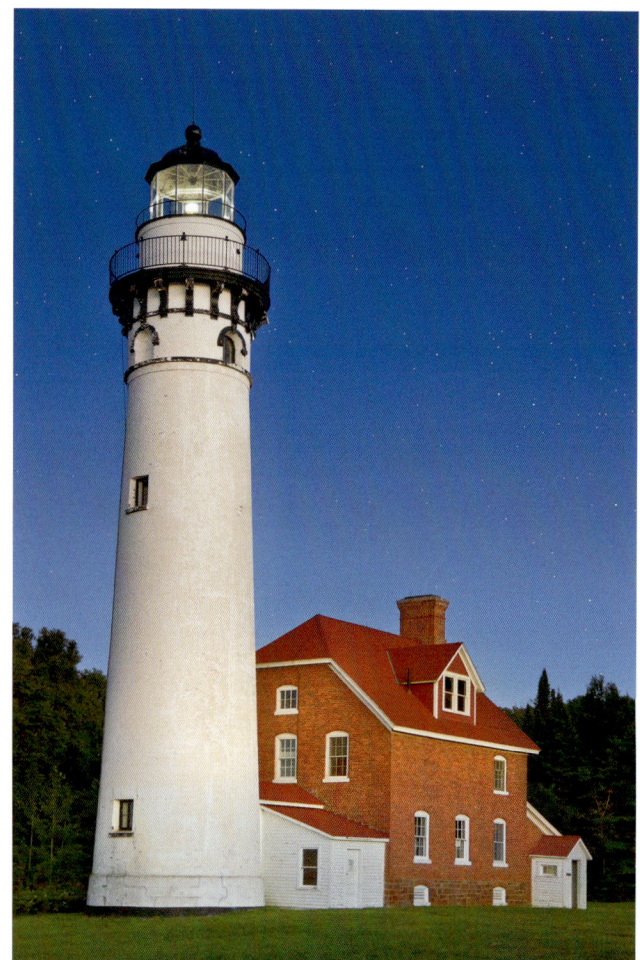
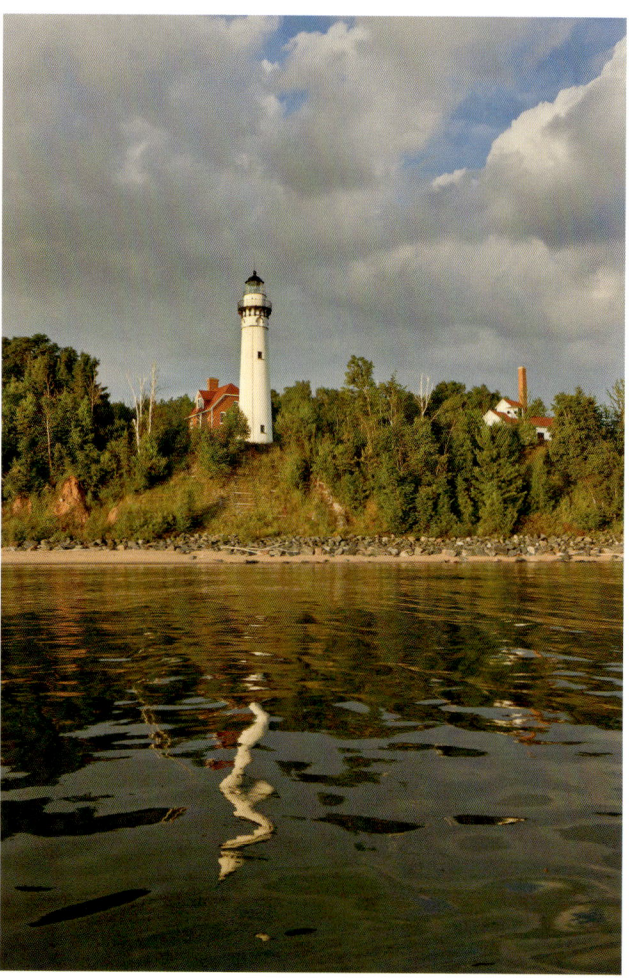

Outer Island Light Station, Apostle Islands National Lakeshore

Plates 31, 32

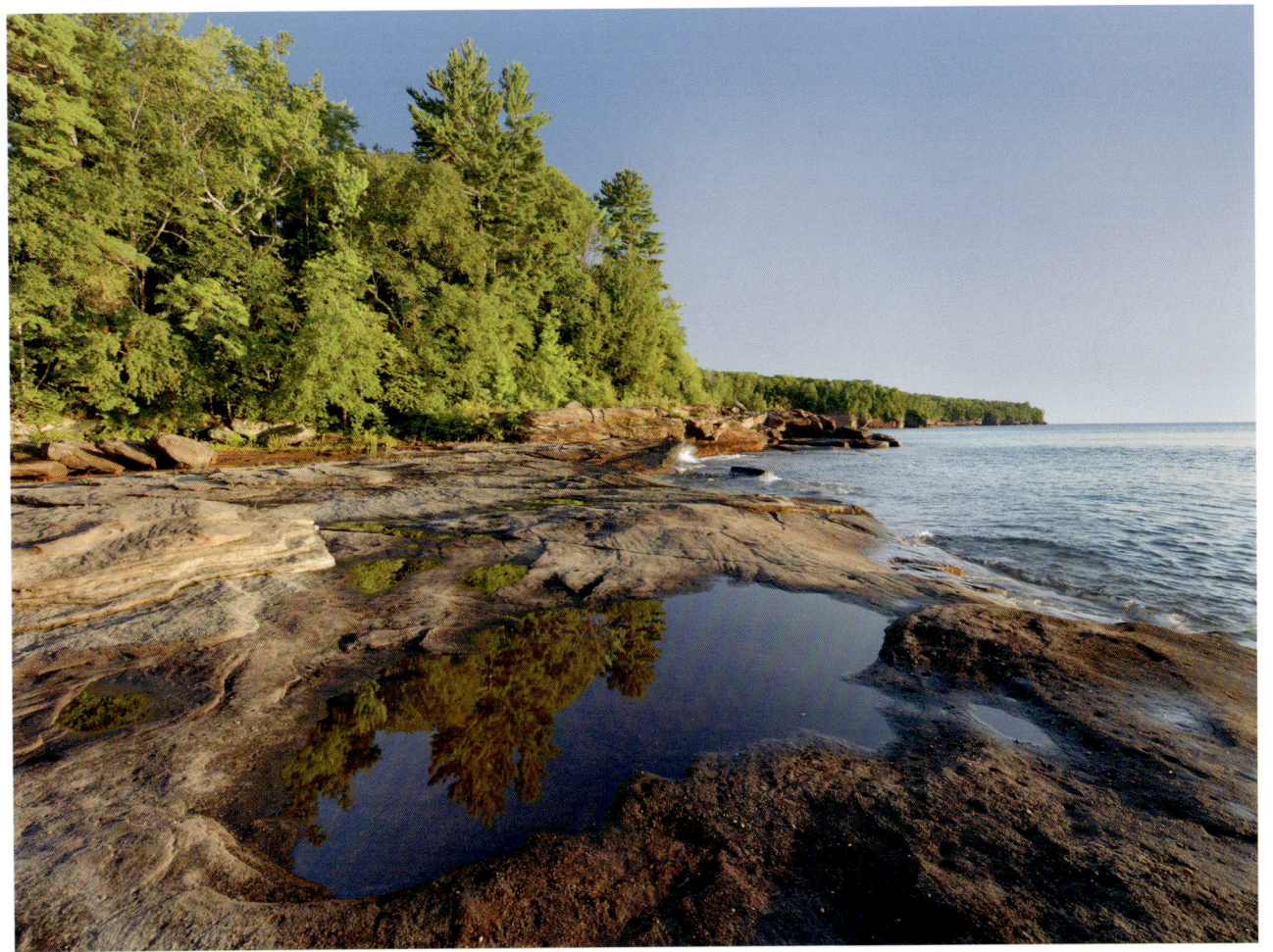

Outer Island, Apostle Islands National Lakeshore

Plate 33

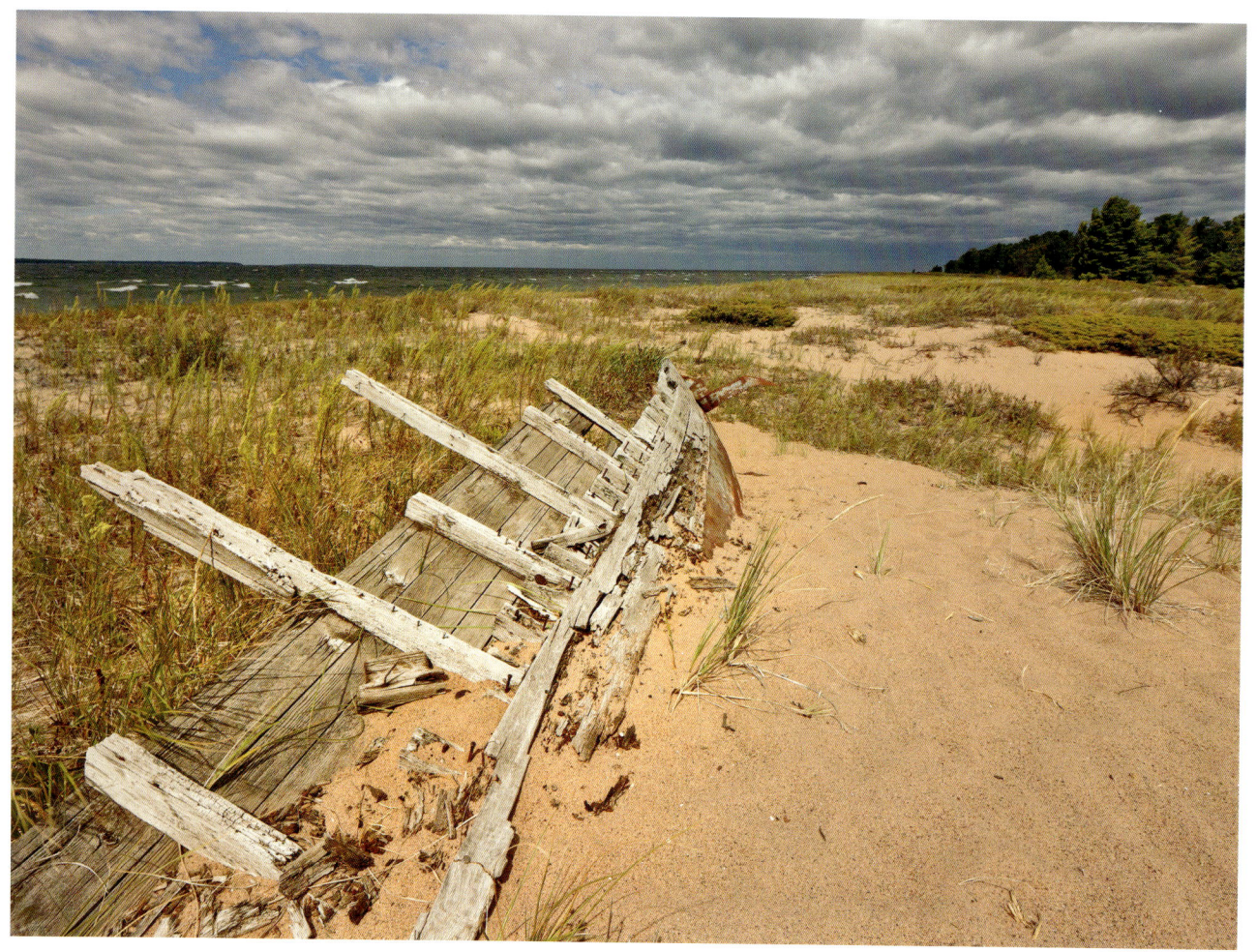

Remains of the tug, Faithful, Outer Island Sand Spit, Apostle Islands National Lakeshore

Plate 34

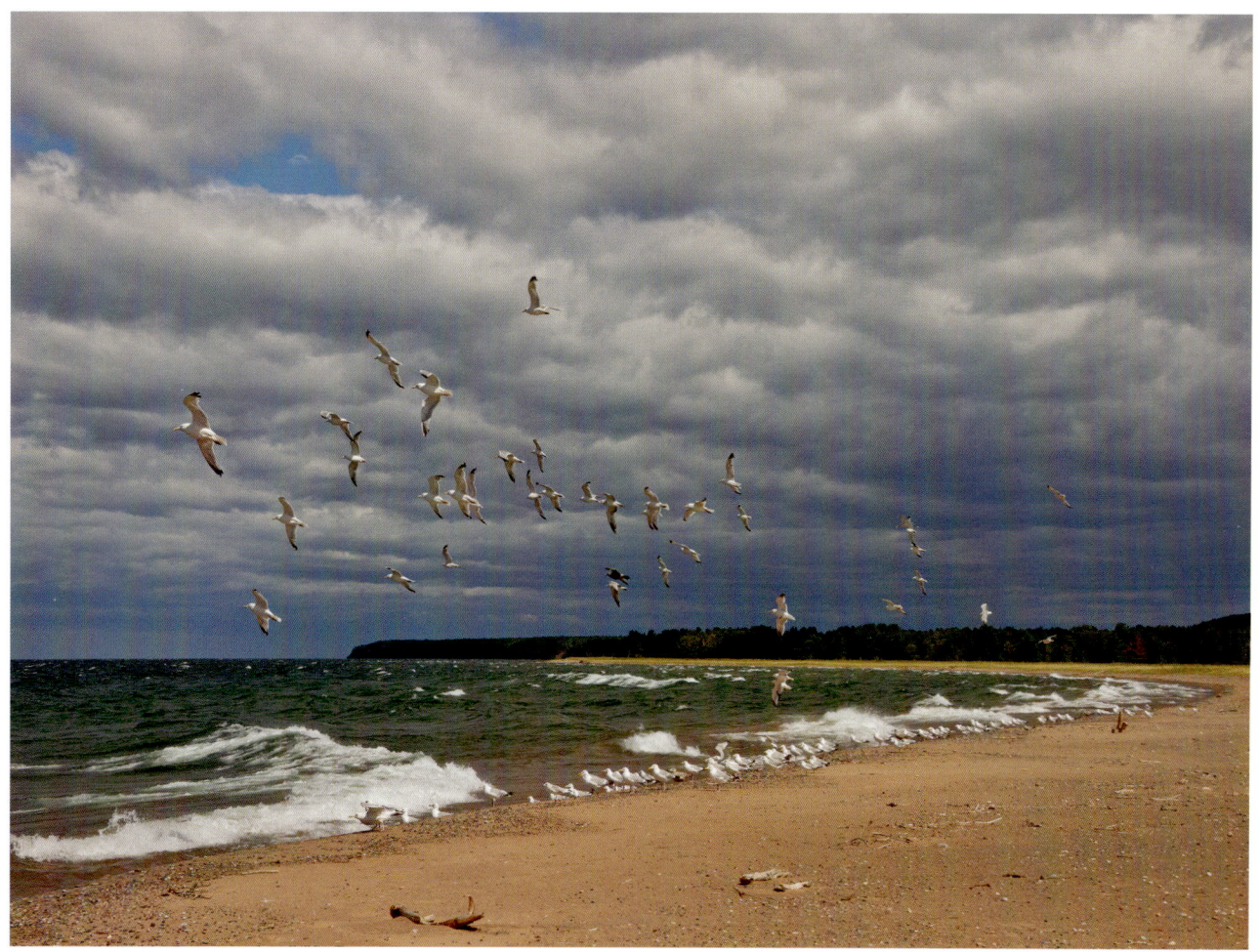

Herring gulls, Outer Island Sand Spit, Apostle Islands National Lakeshore

Plate 35

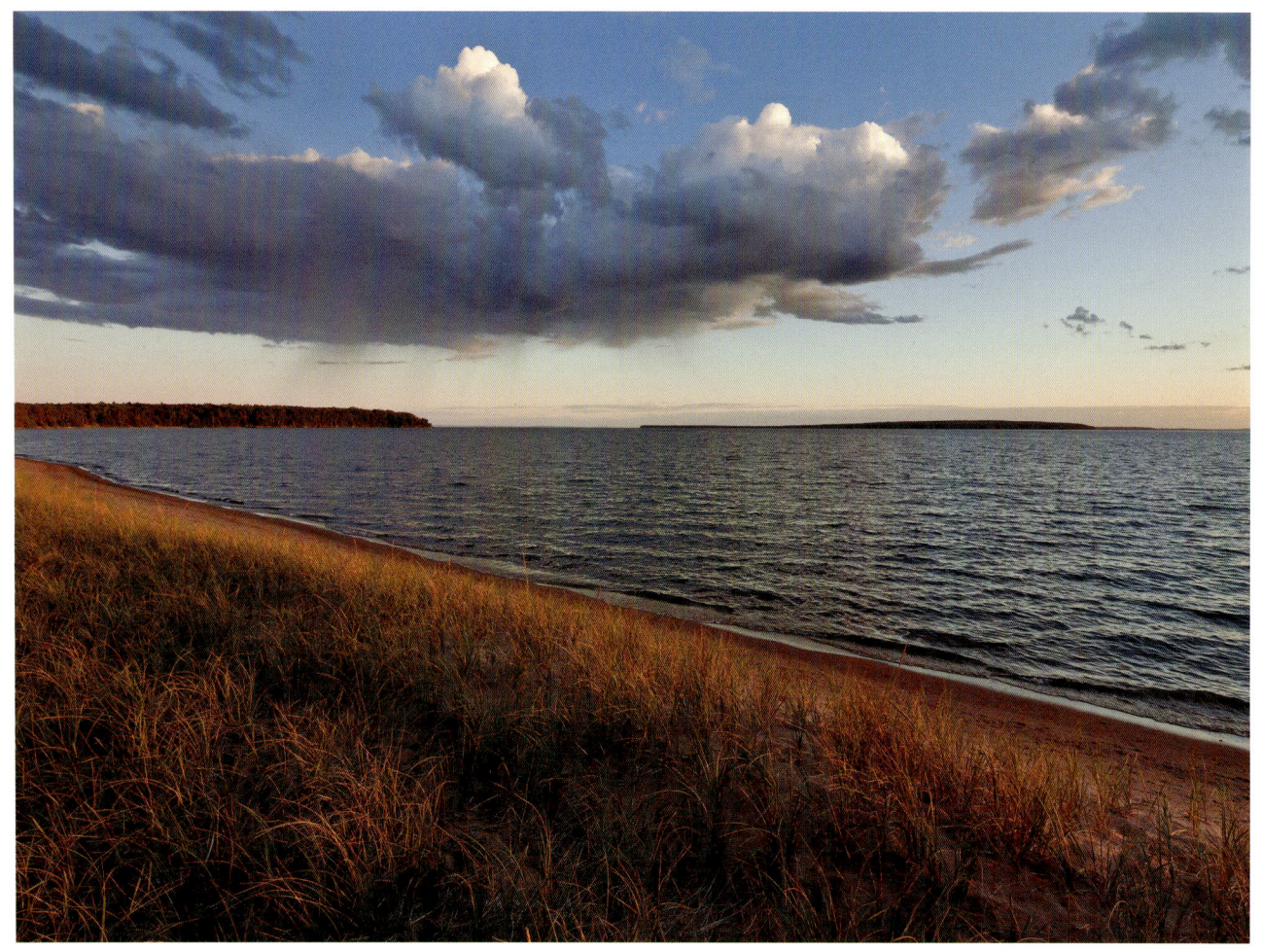

Presque Isle Bay, Stockton Island, Apostle Islands National Lakeshore

Plate 36

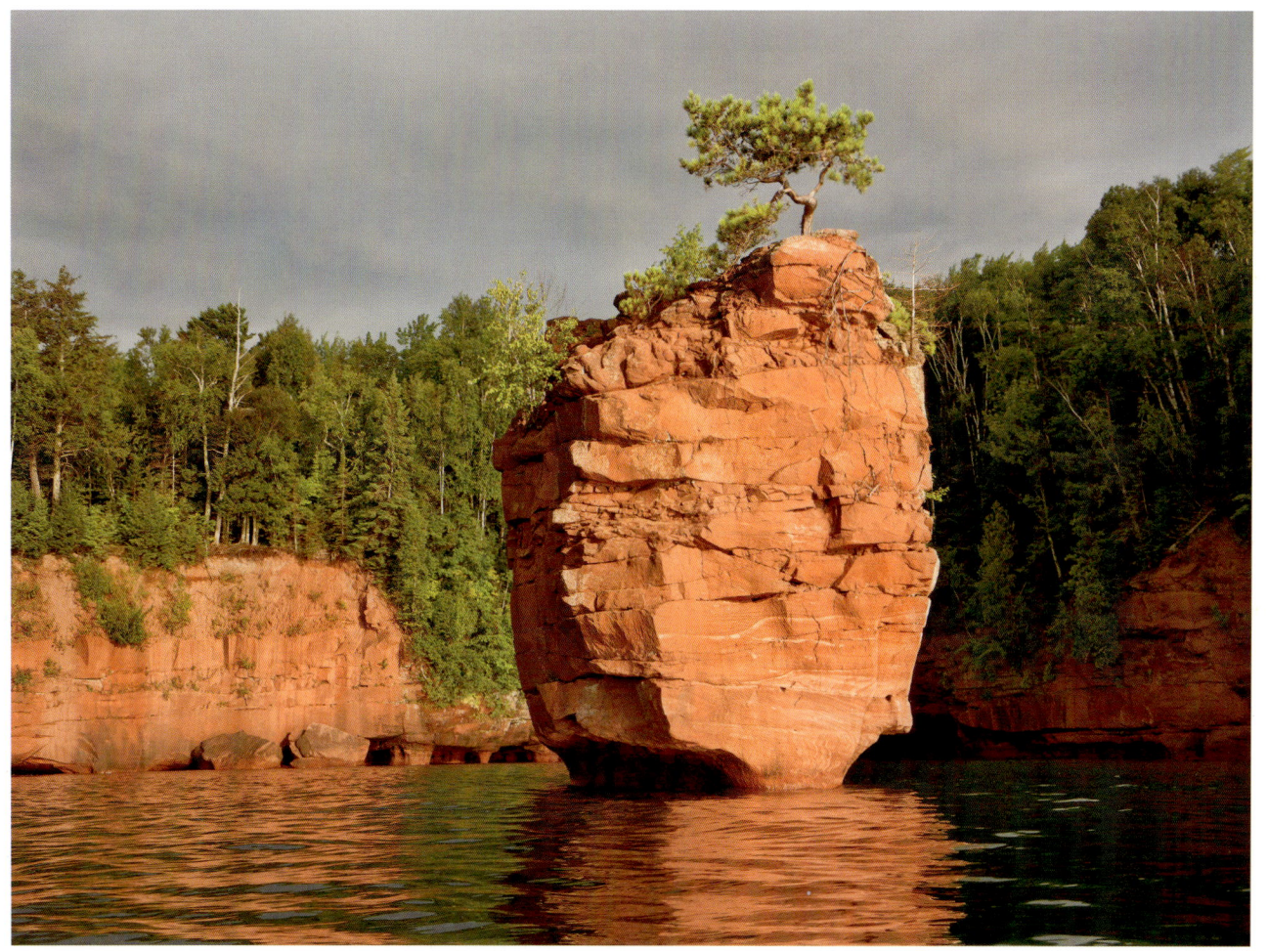

Balancing Rock, Stockton Island, Apostle Islands National Lakeshore

Plate 37

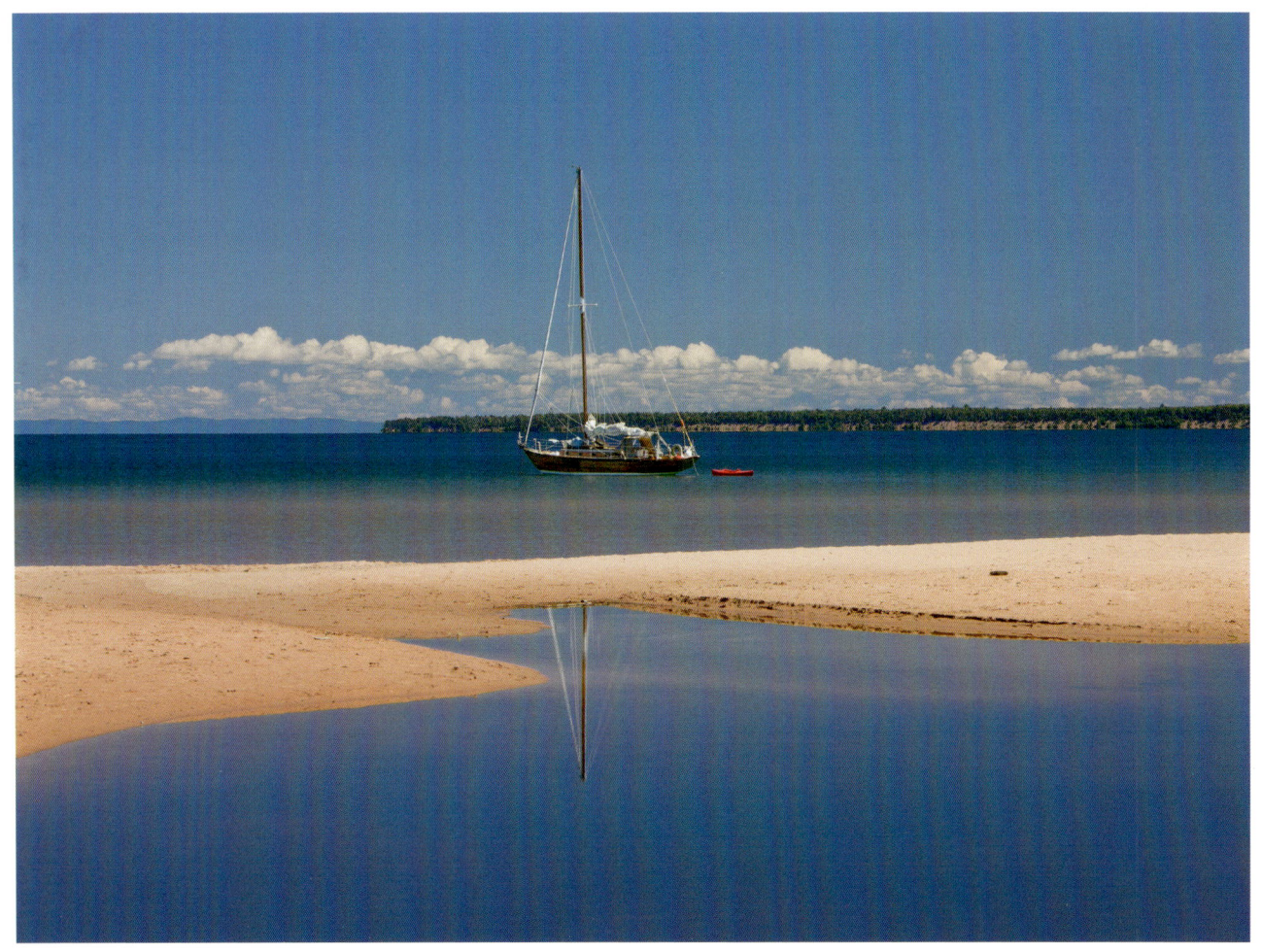

Sailboat anchored at Julian Bay, Stockton Island, Apostle Islands National Lakeshore

Plate 38

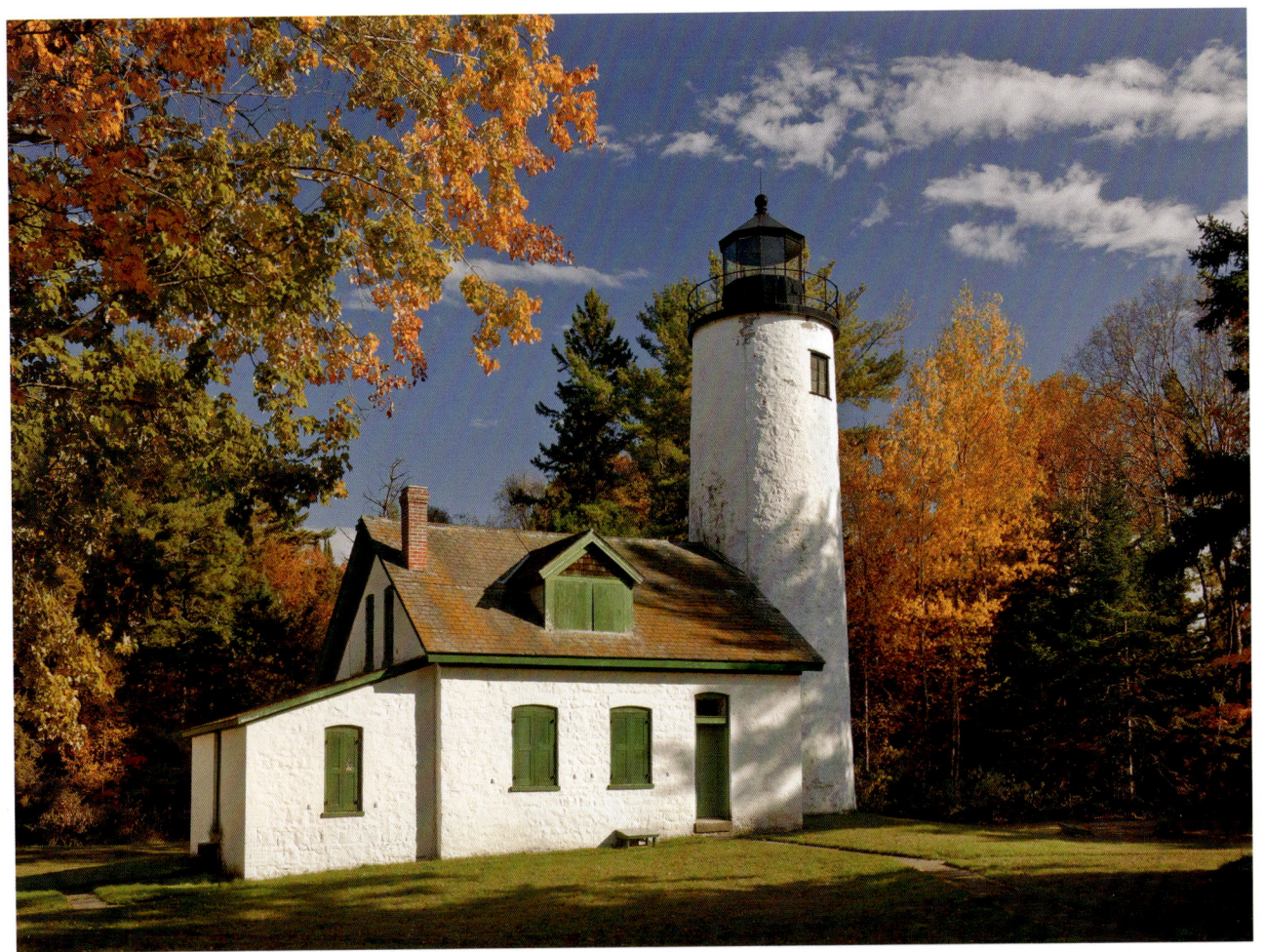

Old Michigan Island Lighthouse, Apostle Islands National Lakeshore

Plate 39

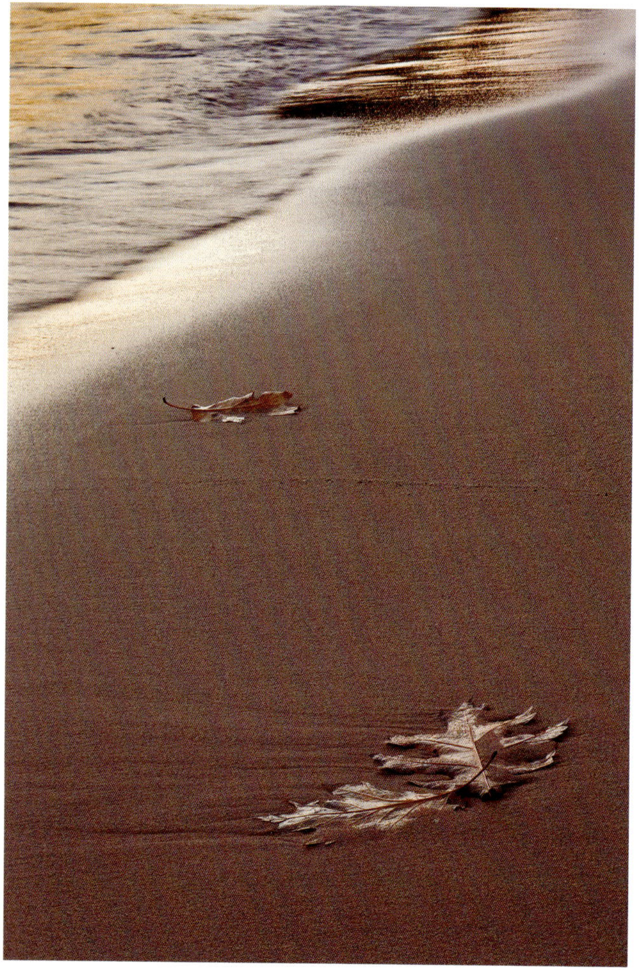

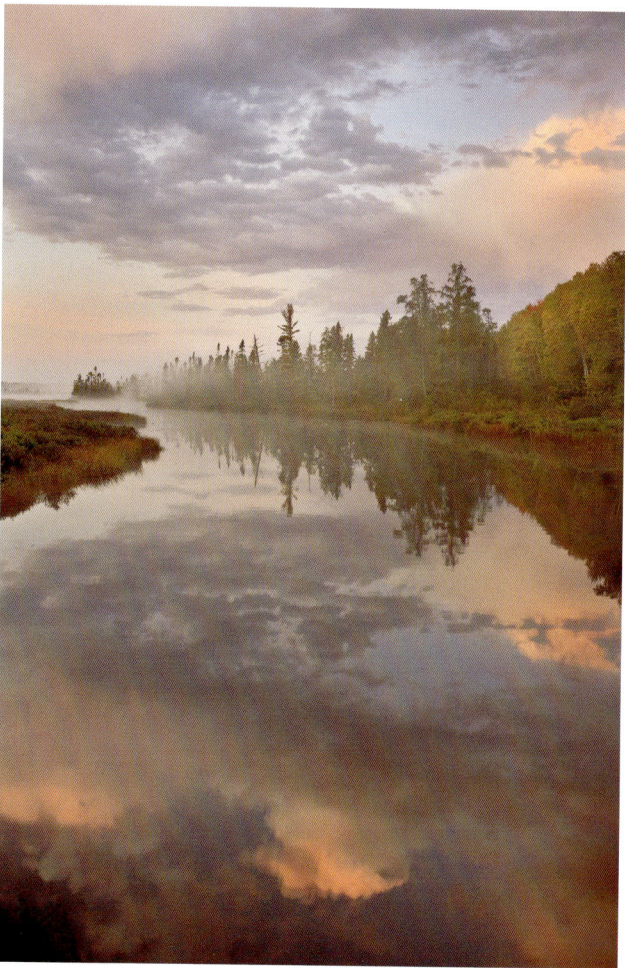

Red oak leaves, Big Bay State Park / Lagoon, Big Bay Town Park, Madeline Island

Plates 40, 41

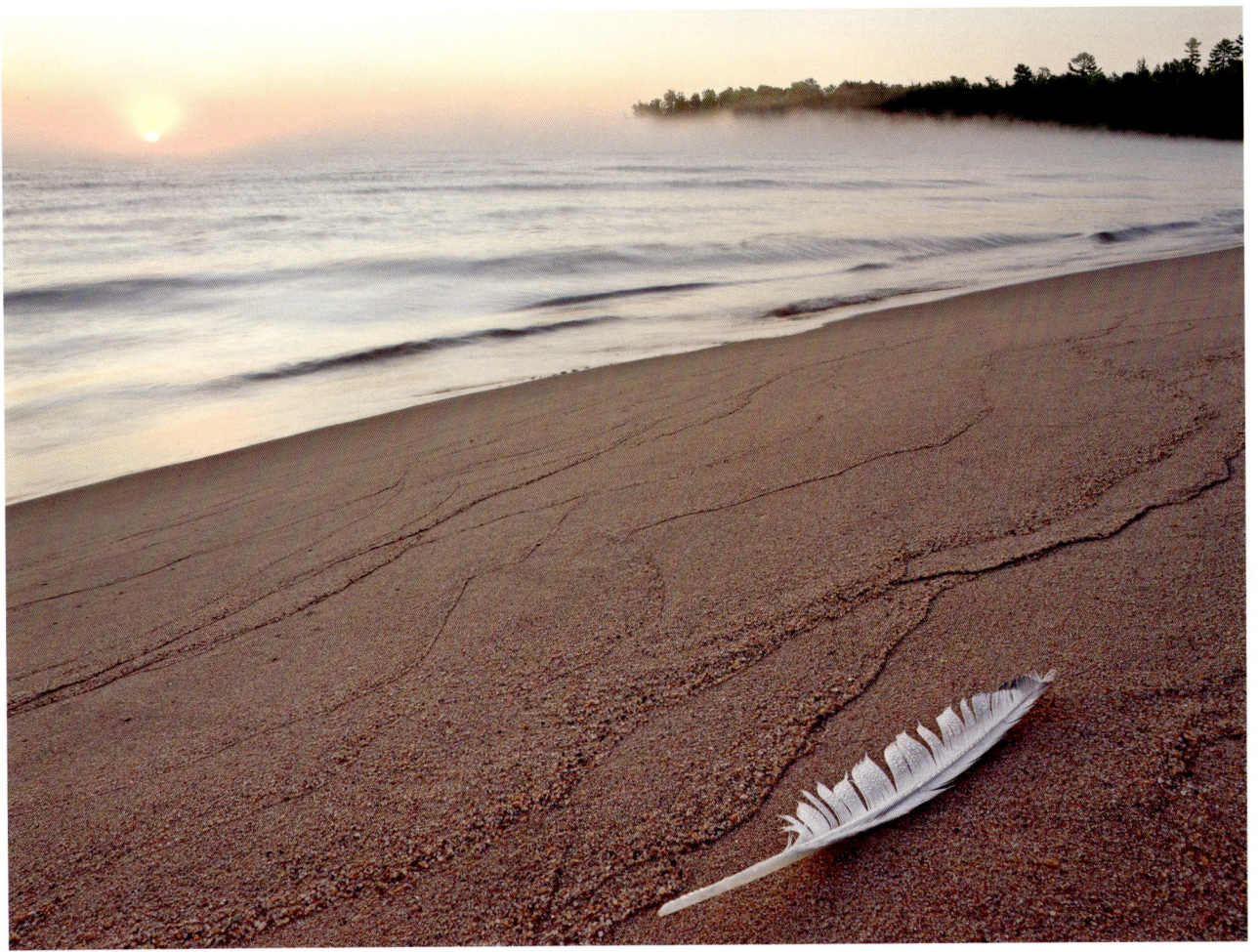

Gull feather, Big Bay State Park, Madeline Island

Plate 42

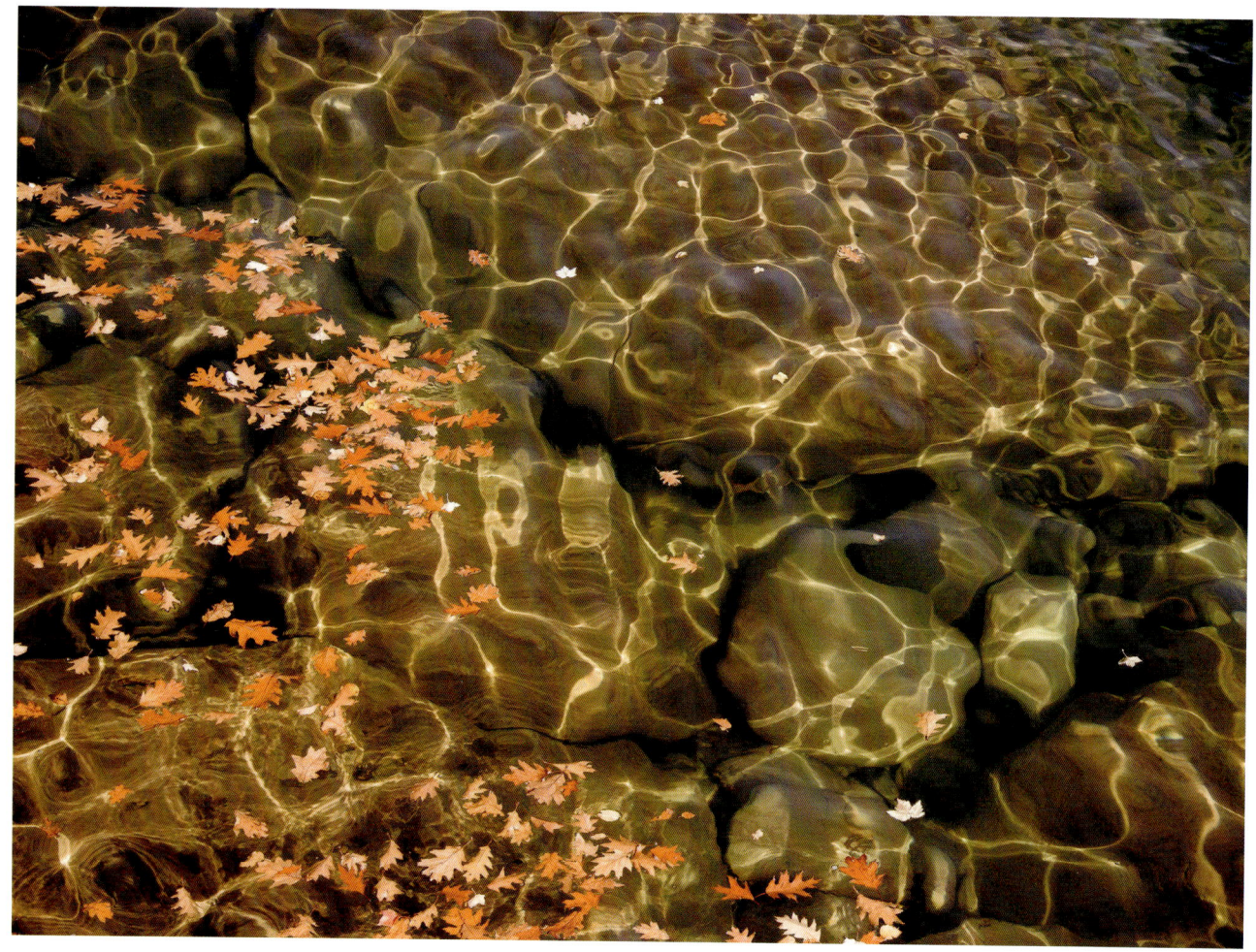

Red oak leaves, Big Bay State Park, Madeline Island

Plate 43

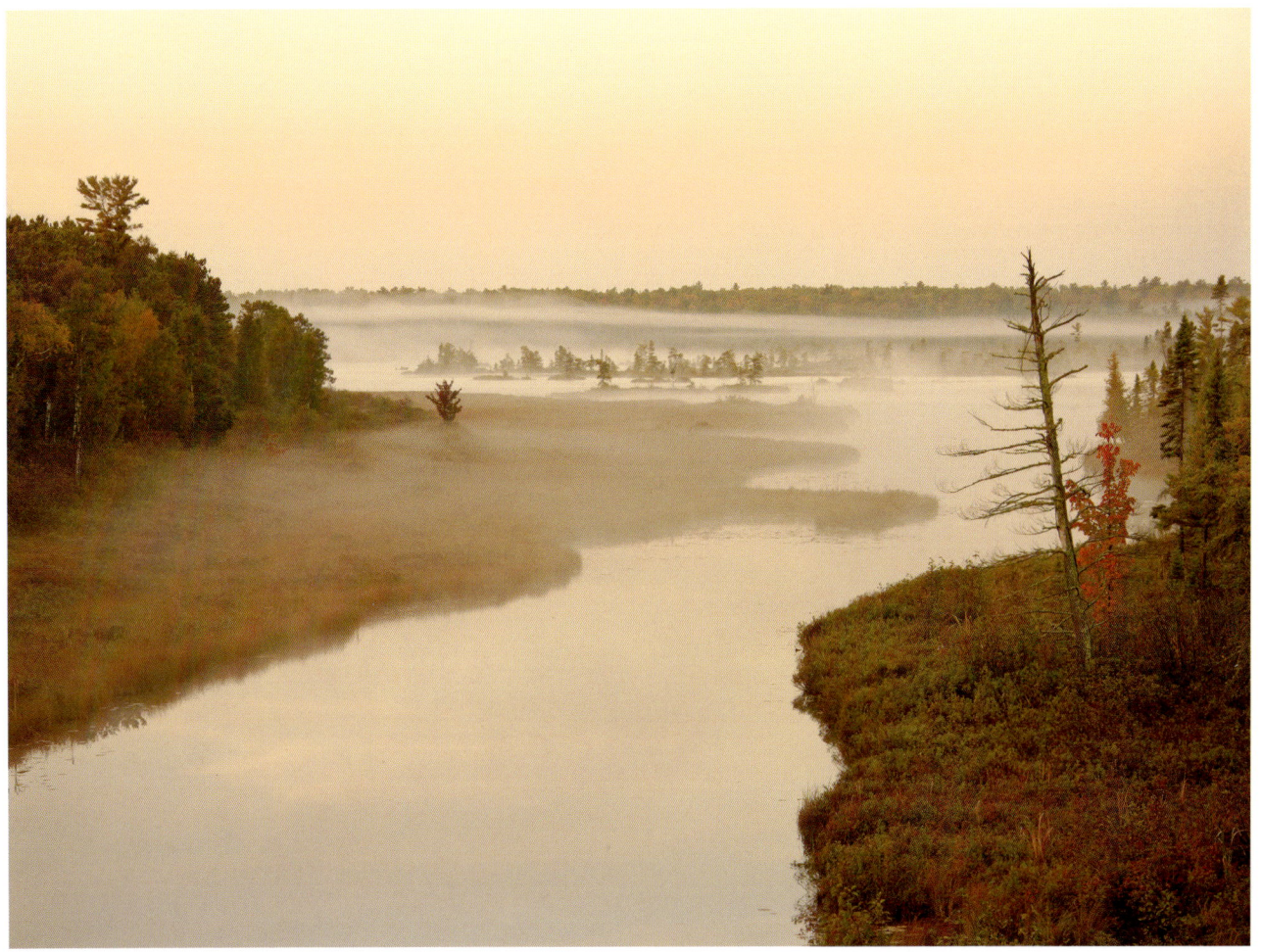

Lagoon, Big Bay Town Park, Madeline Island

Plate 44

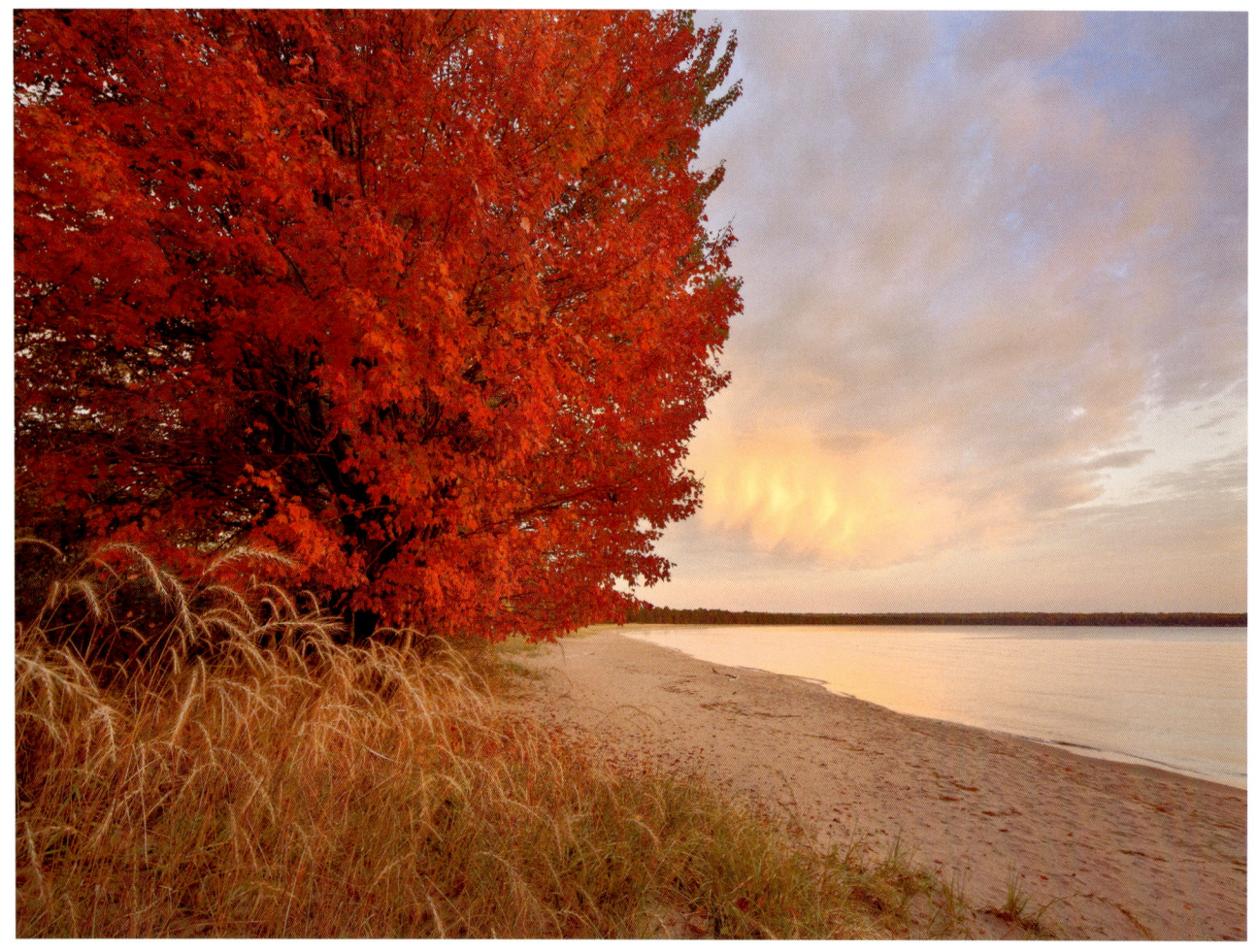

Maple tree and beach grass, Big Bay State Park, Madeline Island

Plate 45

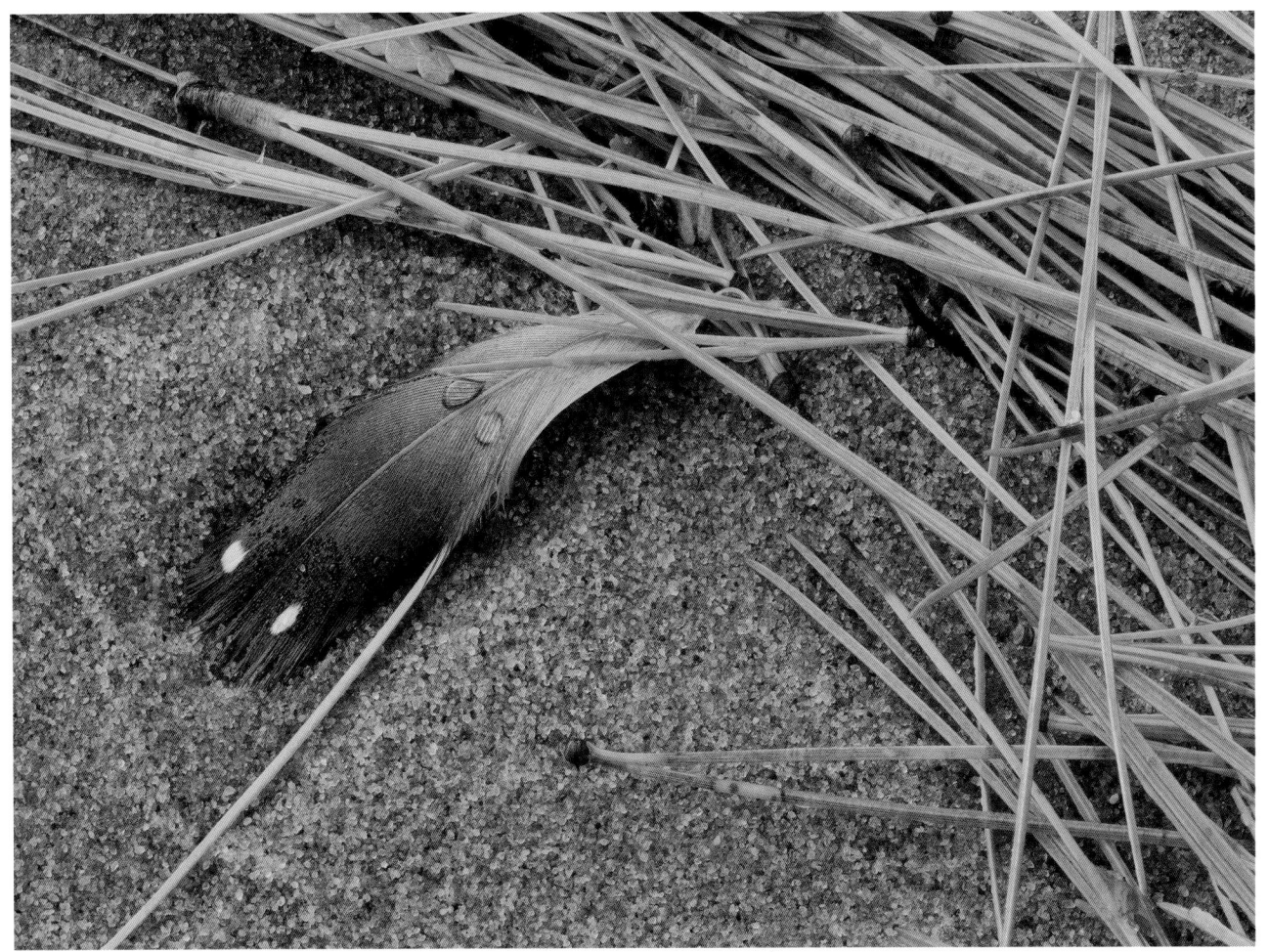

Loon feather and pine needles, Big Bay State Park, Madeline Island

Plate 46